NIKOLAI GUMILEV'S AFRICA

NIKOLAI GUMILEV'S AFRICA

Translated from the Russian by Slava I. Yastremski,

Michael M. Naydan, and Maria Badanova

Edited by Michael M. Naydan

Book cover and interior design by Max Mendor

© 2018, Slava I. Yastremski, Michael M. Naydan, and Maria Badanova

© 2018, Glagoslav Publications

www.glagoslav.com

ISBN: 978-1-91141-463-6

A catalogue record for this book is available from the British Library.

This book is in copyright. No part of this publication may be reproduced, stored in a retrieval system or transmitted in any form or by any means without the prior permission in writing of the publisher, nor be otherwise circulated in any form of binding
or cover other than that in which it is published without a similar condition, including this condition, being imposed
on the subsequent purchaser.

NIKOLAI GUMILEV'S AFRICA

TRANSLATED BY SLAVA I. YASTREMSKI,
MICHAEL M. NAYDAN, AND MARIA BADANOVA

GLAGOSLAV PUBLICATIONS

CONTENTS

INTRODUCTION: ON GUMILEV'S AFRICAN POETRY 9
A NOTE ON THE TRANSLATIONS 13

POETIC WORKS. 15
    FROM *ROMANTIC FLOWERS*, 1908. 16
        THE GARDENS OF MY SOUL. 16
        AN INCANTATION. 17
        A HYENA. 18
        HORROR 19
        THE LION'S BRIDE. 20
        THE PLAGUE. 20
        GIRAFFE 21
        RHINOCEROS 22
        LAKE CHAD. 23
        "FROM THE DISTANT SHORES OF THE NILE…" 25
    FROM *A FOREIGN SKY*, 1912 26
        BY THE FIREPLACE. 26
        ABYSSINIAN SONGS. 28
        I. A WAR SONG 28
        II. FIVE OXEN 28
        III. THE SLAVES' SONG 30
        IV. THE WOMEN OF ZANZIBAR 30
    FROM *THE QUIVER*, 1915 32
        AN AFRICAN NIGHT 32

FROM *THE BONFIRE*, 1918 33
    THE AZBAKIYA 33
THE TENT, 1921 35
    INTRODUCTION 35
    THE RED SEA 36
    EGYPT 38
    THE SAHARA 42
    THE SUEZ CANAL 45
    SUDAN 47
    ABYSSINIA 50
    THE GALLA 53
    THE SOMALI PENINSULA 55
    LIBERIA 56
    MADAGASCAR 59
    ZAMBEZI 60
    THE DAMARA 63
    EQUATORIAL FOREST 64
    DAHOMEY 67
    THE NIGER 68
FROM *THE PILLAR OF FIRE*, 1921 70
    A LEOPARD 70
FROM *UNCOLLECTED WORKS* 72
    <AN ACROSTIC> 72
    A POEM TO THE MUSIC OF DAVYDOV 73
    "PALM TREES, THREE ELEPHANTS, AND TWO GIRAFFES..." 73
    CHRISTMAS IN ABYSSINIA 74
    ALGIERS AND TUNIS 75
    ABYSSINIAN SONGS 78
    "ONE CANNOT ESCAPE DEATH:
    THERE ONCE WAS AN EMPEROR ABA-DANYA..." 78
    "THIS NIGHT I SAW A CAT IN MY DREAM..." 79

"MENELIK SAID: "I LOVE THOSE WHO SADDLE..." 79

"THE ATTACKING WARRIOR IS
AS STRONG AS A PILLAR..." 80

"THE GREATEST JOY IS TO WATCH..." 80

"THERE IS FIRE IN THE NEGUS'S RIFLE..." 81

"AS PEOPLE, UPON SEEING LIEGE IYASSU,
TREMBLE WITH FEAR..." 81

"HOI, HOI, ABA-MULAT HAILE GEORGI..." 82

"ONE WHO KILLS A LION IS GREATER
THAN ONE WHO KILLS AN ELEPHANT..." 82

"HUME AND DAGOME TOGETHER
OWN THE WORLD-STONE..." 83

PROSE WRITINGS 85

PRINCESS ZARA 86

THE FOREST DEVIL 91

THE AFRICAN HUNT 98

UPSTREAM ALONG THE NILE 107

HAS MENELIK DIED? 110

THE AFRICAN DIARY 113

AFRICAN DIARY 2 142

UNDER THE UNNECESSARY NET OF LONGITUDES
AND LATITUDES: THE PROBLEM OF THE RELATIONSHIP
BETWEEN MAN AND SPACE IN NIKOLAI GUMILEV'S
AFRICAN PHOTOGRAPHS 155

THE PHOTOGRAPHS FROM
THE GUMILEV AFRICA EXPEDITIONS 167

Nikolai Gumilev

1886—1921

INTRODUCTION:
ON GUMILEV'S AFRICAN POETRY

Western readers perhaps know Nikolai Gumilev primarily as the husband of the great Russian poet Anna Akhmatova. In his time Gumilev was a recognized poet, one of the most important figures in the culture of the Silver Age in Russia, even before his marriage to Akhmatova (who incidentally was not yet an established poet when they married). He was the founder of Russian literary Acmeism, which comes from the French word *acme*, meaning the summit or pinnacle. Along with Symbolism and Futurism, Acmeism comprised one of the three most significant poetic movements in early twentieth-century Russia and focused on "beautiful clarity" (the poet Mikhail Kuzmin coined) and simplicity of expression instead of the profoundly complex and symbolic nature of the word in Symbolism, one of Acmeism's immediate literary predecessors. In addition to Gumilev and Akhmatova, the major Acmeists included Osip Mandelstam, Sergei Gorodetsky, Georgy Adamovich, as well as a few others. To differentiate Gumilev from the other Acmeists, one can characterize his poetry by its vivid imagery, bright colors, and exotic locales that entered his poems from numerous travels to France, Italy, England, and, what became most important to him, Africa. The poet rightly called the source of his creativity the Muse of Distant Travels.

Gumilev's life was as bright and fascinating as his art. In fact his biography often overshadowed his achievements as a poet. The critical moment that defined his biography was his execution in August 1921 on charges he participated in a counterrevolutionary conspiracy. In recent years those charges were proven to have been completely false and fabricated by the Soviet secret police. Gumilev was the first major artistic figure to fall victim to the Soviet regime, and his name, especially in immigrant circles, became a symbol of resistance to Soviet totalitarianism, despite the fact that political motifs occupied a very modest place in his writings.

What distinguishes Gumilev not only from other poets of his generation but indeed places him in a unique position in the history of

Russian poetry is his profound involvement with Africa. He extensively wrote both poetry and prose, on the culture of the continent in general and on Ethiopia (Abyssinia, as it was called in Gumilev's time) in particular. During Gumilev's abbreviated lifetime he made four trips to Northern and Eastern Africa, the most extensive of which was an April-August 1913 expedition to Abyssinia undertaken on assignment from the St. Petersburg Imperial Museum of Anthropology and Ethnography. During that trip Gumilev collected Ethiopian folklore and ethnographic objects, which, upon his return to St. Petersburg, he deposited at the Museum. He and his assistant Nikolai Sverchkov also made more than 200 photographs that offer a unique picture of the African country in the early part of the century.

African motifs began to appear very early in Gumilev's poetry, even before he actually visited the continent. According to Gumilev's own personal assessment, his first "acceptable" collection *Romantic Flowers* (1908) contains poems thematically centered around Lake Chad, which, at that time the poet associated with the heart of mysterious Black Africa. For the most part his treatment of Africa in the poems from this collection is affected by Gumilev's favorite writers of that time – Jules Verne, Captain Mayne Reid, and especially Ryder Haggard. The poem "Incantation," for example, is directly based on Haggard's novel *Cleopatra*, particularly on the scene in which the priest Harmahis shows Cleopatra (who usurped his throne) the mysteries of the Egyptian gods. In this poem we also find the image of the "pillars of fire" that later will become the title of Gumilev's last collection of poetry (published posthumously in 1921). Gumilev's poem "Giraffe" became the cornerstone of this collection and became Gumilev's trademark in bohemian circles of pre-war (WWI) St. Petersburg. On the whole the African imagery in *Romantic Flowers* is somewhat abstract and closely resembles the pictures of British Pre-Raphaelites and Russian Art Nouveau artists. In the collection Gumilev idealized Africa as an exotic Orient.

The collection *A Foreign Sky* marks a change in Gumilev's treatment of the African theme in his works. The change was undoubtedly caused by the poet's immediate experience on the so-called Dark Continent. By the time he published the collection Gumilev had made two trips to Africa – a brief one to Egypt in 1908 and a much longer one to Abyssinia in 1910. His poems after those two journeys include actual details of African nature and Gumilev's own engagement with it. In the poem "Ezbekiya" from the 1918 collection *The Quiver* Gumilev reflects on his visit to the Cairo garden in 1908. At that time he was preoccupied with thoughts of suicide because of Anna Akhmatova's rejection of his marriage proposal, which she subsequently accepted two years later. The visit to the Ezbekiya garden healed Gumilev spiritually, and all his future trips to Africa had the same beneficial effect on his state of mind and inspired him artistically.

The collection *The Tent* (1921) became the most significant among Gumilev's poetic works on Africa and was published a few months before his execution. It consists entirely of poems dedicated to Africa. As his wife Anna Akhmatova noted in her memoirs, *The Tent* is a book of geography in verse. This statement is supported by the memoirs of the Russian explorer of Africa V. I. Nemirovich-Danchenko to whom Gumilev said in 1921: "I am writing a geography in verse. It is the most poetic of all the sciences but people make some kind of herbarium out of it. I am now working on Africa, the black African tribes. I must show how they imagined the world for themselves." The plan for a large poetic book of a "geography in verse" was discovered among Gumilev's archival papers. It consisted of six sections: Europe, Asia, Africa, America, and Australia. The outline of the African section showed that Gumilev intended to write his poems in correspondence to an imaginary trip around Africa, starting with Egypt, then following the Western coast of the continent, and ending the journey at the Red Sea. It must be noted that the journey, with the exception of its beginning and the very end, would take place in locations where Gumilev had never been. In comparison with this plan, *The Tent* consists almost entirely of poems dedicated to those places in Africa that Gumilev visited several times, the central of which comprises the area of the Horn of Africa that includes Abyssinia, Galla, Somalia, the Red Sea, and adjacent to the latter, Egypt and Sudan.

Gumilev visited Abyssinia at the end of the reign of the country's great leader Menelik II, who in 1896 defeated the Italian army at the river Adwa and won independence for Abyssinia, which was the only uncolonized African country at the end of the 19th century. It had a special appeal for Russia (which didn't participate in the "scramble for Africa") because of the shared with Ethiopia Eastern Orthodox religion. Gumilev's poems include many references to the history of Ethiopia – from the legendary Axum empire to the times of the more recent military and government leaders such as Ras Mekonnen and the prophet Sheik Hussein – as well as some comments on the modern social issues of the country, such as the conflict between the indigenous population and the Europeans. In the collection *The Tent*, Gumilev's African landscape becomes as real as the people who populate it. The poet includes his personal recollections of traveling through various parts of Abyssinia, and in descriptions of those parts of Africa where he was not able to go, he proceeds from concrete visual imagery: maps, pictures, and actual artifacts, as is evident in the last poem of the collection "The Niger."

In sum in retrospect we cannot consider Gumilev to have been a "politically correct" writer in regard to his writings on Africa. His views certainly can be characterized as "Orientalist" by present-day standards. However, his African-themed poems bear the stamp of not only his genuine love and understanding of different independent African cultures but also of an actual merging with at least one of them and depicting it from within, from the point of view of a participant.

Slava I. Yastremski
Professor of Russian Bucknell University

A NOTE ON THE TRANSLATIONS

This edition for the first time compiles virtually all of Nikolai Gumilev's Africa-themed works (poems, prose, and diaries) in a single volume in English translation along with a number of extant photographs from the Gumilev archive in Russia. I have stuck to Slava's outline and design for the book, which has been a longtime labor of love for him. Many of the translations are appearing in English for the first time.[1] After my co-translator Slava Yastremski succumbed to illness in November 2015, I was able to download all his materials on Gumilev from his laptop thanks to Slava's widow Irina, who was kind enough to give me access. She also gave me the photographs from Gumilev's African travels that Slava had obtained earlier from the Gumilev archive in Russia for publication in this volume. Given the age of the photographs and Gumilev's death in 1921, all these works lie in the public domain. While Slava's and my translations were approaching completion when he died, he was too weak to do a final edit the months before he passed away. Therefore I have decided to include an edit by my very talented honors college undergraduate student at Penn State Maria Badanova, who did a marvelous job in checking and editing this final manuscript and improving it. I am grateful to Laird Jones for sharing his expertise on Africa with me for this volume. I am responsible for any errors or omissions that might have slipped through. I have decided to use English equivalents of words that Gumilev uses such as "Negro" (negr) and "dwarf" (karlik) instead of versions of those words preferred in contemporary English usage to keep to the style of colonial usage extant in the poet's time.

Michael M. Naydan
Woskob Family Professor of Ukrainian Studies and
Professor of Slavic Languages and Literatures
The Pennsylvania State University

---

[1] Burton Raffel's and Alla Burago's translations were published in *Selected Works of Nikolai S. Gumilev* (Albany: SUNY Albany Press, 1972). The volume includes just a handful of Gumilev's African poems and three of his prose works on the subject.

POETIC WORKS

FROM *ROMANTIC FLOWERS*, 1908

THE GARDENS OF MY SOUL

The gardens of my soul are always filled with patterns,
In them the winds are so fresh and blow so softly,
In them you find golden sands and black marble,
And pools that are deep and entirely translucent.

In them, just as in a dream, plants are extraordinary,
Birds glow pink like water in the morning
And—who can understand the clue to an age-old secret?—
In them, there is a maiden wearing a High Priestess' wreath.

Her eyes are like the reflections of pure gray steel,
Her graceful brow is whiter than eastern lilies.
She has lips that have kissed no one
And that have never uttered a word to anyone.

Her cheeks are pinkish pearls of the South,
The treasure of unthinkable fantasies,
Her hands that have only caressed one another
When intertwined in the ecstasy of prayer.

By her feet, there are two black panthers
With a metallic tint to their fur,
And flying up from the rose bushes of a secret grotto
Her pink flamingoes float in the azure.

I do not look at the world of streaming lines,
My dreams are obedient to nothing but the eternal.
Let fierce sirocco winds rage in the desert,
The gardens of my soul are always filled with patterns.

AN INCANTATION

The young magician in a purple tunic
Spoke mysterious words
Before her, the queen of lawlessness,
He squandered rubies of magic.

The aroma of the burning incense
Opened spaces that knew no limits
Where gloomy shadows were rushing,
Looking like fish, then like birds.

Invisible strings gently sobbed,
Pillars of fire floated in the air,
Proud military tribunes submissively
Lowered their eyes like slaves.

And the queen disturbed these mysteries,
Playing with the loftiness of the universe,
And her silky-smooth skin
Intoxicated him with its snowy whiteness.

Yielding to the power of her whims,
The young magician forgot everything around him,
Looking at her small breasts,
At the bracelets on her outstretched arms.

The young magician in the purple tunic
Spoke without a breath, like the dead,
He gave the queen of transgressions
All that made his soul feel alive.

And when the crescent moon began to sway
On the emeralds of the Nile and faded,
The pale-faced queen tossed
The flower glowing crimson for him.

A HYENA

Over the reeds of the sluggish Nile
Where only butterflies and birds fly,
A forgotten grave is hidden
Of a lawless but alluring queen.

The darkness of the night brings its tricks,
The moon arises like a sinful siren,
Whitish mists are spreading fast,
And a hyena is stealing out from its lair.

Its groaning is furious and vulgar,
Its eyes are sinister and gloomy,
And frightful are her bared teeth
On the pinkish marble of a grave.

"Look, moon, a lover of the reckless,
Look, stars, you beautiful visions,
And you dark Nile, the master of quiet water,
And you, birds, butterflies, and plants.

Look everyone, how my fur stands on end,
How my eyes gleam with evil fires,
Isn't it true that I am, too, a queen
Like the one who sleeps beneath these stones?

Her heart once was beating full of betrayal,
Her arched eyebrows used to bring death,
She was the same hyena as I am,
She, like I, loved the smell of blood."

In villages, dogs howl full of fear.
Little children cry in their homes,
And stern *fellahs*[2] grasp
Their long, merciless whips in their hands.

---

2   *Fellah* – a name for a farmer in Ancient Egypt.

HORROR

I walked through corridors for a long time,
Around me silence lurked like an enemy.
Statues watched the intruder
From their niches with a hostile gaze.

Objects were frozen in some gloomy dream,
And strange was the gray twilight,
And like a foreboding pendulum
My lonely steps resounded.

And there where the dreary dusk was darker,
My blazing gaze was disturbed
By a barely visible figure
In the shadow of crowded columns.

I approached, and in an instant
Fear clawed at me like a beast:
I met the head of a hyena
On shapely maiden's shoulders.

Blood was smeared on her sharp muzzle,
Her eyes were a gaping void,
And a vile hoarse whisper crept out:
"You've come here on your own, you are mine!"

Terrible minutes flew past,
And the gloaming spread,
While countless mirrors
Repeated the pale horror.

THE LION'S BRIDE

The priest made the decision. The people,
In agreement with him, knifed my mother:
A desert lion, a handsome god,
Waits for me in the savanna Paradise.

I am not fearful, would I hide
From the threatening enemy?
I put on a crimson sash,
Amber and pearls.

And here in the desert I cry out:
"Sun-beast, you have kept me waiting,
Come to rend into pieces
The human prey, my prince!

Let me shudder in your heavy paws,
Let me fall and not rise again,
Let me smell the terrifying odor,
Dark and intoxicating, like love."

Grasses have the odor of incense,
I am quiet as a bride,
Above me is the murderous
Of my gold-colored groom.

THE PLAGUE

A ship is approaching Cairo
With the long banners of the Prophet.
Looking at the sailors, it is easy to see
They are from the East.

The captain shouts and scurries about,
His voice is guttural and raspy,

Swarthy faces and red fezzes
Can be seen in the rigging.

Children crowd on the pier,
Their thin bodies look comical,
They have gathered here at dawn
To see where the visitors will dock.

Storks sit on the roofs
And crane their necks.
They are higher than anyone else
And they can see better.

Storks are airborne magicians,
They understand many secret things:
For example, why one vagrant
Has purple spots on his cheeks.

Storks chatter above the houses,
But no one hears that they say:
Alongside perfume and silk
Plague makes its way into the city.

GIRAFFE

Today I can see your gaze is especially sad,
And your arms are especially lean, hugging your knees
Listen, my love: far off by Lake Chad
An elegant giraffe is roaming.

It is graciously slender and slight
And its skin adorned with a magical pattern
That can be rivaled only by the moon's glimmer
Rippling and swaying on the surface of spacious lakes.

From afar, it resembles the colorful sails of a ship,
And its stride is smooth like the flight of a happy bird.
I am certain the earth sees many wondrous things
When at twilight the giraffe hides in its marble cavern.

I know joyful tales of mysterious lands
About a black maiden and the passion of a young chief,
But you've been breathing the heavy mist for too long,
You don't want to believe in anything but the rain.

How can I tell you about a tropical garden,
About slender palm trees, and the smell of unimaginable herbs?
You're crying? Listen… far off by Lake Chad
An elegant giraffe is roaming.

RHINOCEROS

Do you see monkeys scurrying,
Screaming wildly, in the vines
That hang, oh, so low,
Do you hear the shuffle of many feet?
That means—very close to
Your forest clearing
An enraged rhino is lurking.

Do you see the general commotion,
Do you hear the trampling? There's no doubt
If even the sleepy bison
Are retreating deeper into the mud.
But, since you are in love with the mystical,
Do not look for your salvation
In running away or hiding.

Raise your arms high
In a song of happiness and parting,
Glances, covered with pink mists,

Will lead your thoughts far into the distance,
And from the promised lands
Feluccas[3] invisible to us
Will sail in to carry you away.

LAKE CHAD

On mysterious Lake Chad
Among the ancient baobabs,
At dawn carved *feluccas*
Swiftly carry majestic Arabs.
Along the lake's wooded shores,
And by the green foot of the mountains
Maiden priestesses with ebony skin
Worship terrifying gods.

I was the wife of a powerful chief,
A daughter of imperious Lake Chad,
During winter rain I alone
Performed the mysterious rites.
They used to say that within a hundred miles
There wasn't a woman more fair than I,
I never took the bracelets off my wrists,
And amber always dangled on my neck.

My white warrior was so graceful,
His lips so red, his gaze so calm.
He was a true chief;
And a door opened in my heart,
And when the heart whispers to us,
We don't struggle, we don't wait.
He said they hardly
Saw anyone in France
Who was more seductive than me;

---

[3] *Felucca* – a light boat.

    And as soon as this day melts away,
    He would saddle
    A Berber steed for the two of us.

My husband chased us with his trusty bow,
Running through forest thickets,
Jumping over ravines,
Swimming across dusky lakes,
And death's terror fell on him.
Only the scorching day saw
The corpse of the ferocious wanderer,
The one covered with shame.

    And, astride a fast and powerful camel,
    Drowning in a caressing pile
    Of animal skins and silk,
    I flew like a bird, to the north.
    I broke my exquisite fan,
    Reveling in ecstasy, in anticipation,
    I parted the supple folds
    Of my many-colored tent
    And, laughing, leaned into the window,
    I watched the sun dance
    In the blue eyes of the European.

And now I am like a dead sycamore
That has shed all of its leaves,
I am an unwanted, dreary lover,
Like a thing, I am cast aside in Marseilles.
To feed on pitiful refuse,
To live, in the evening
I dance for drunken sailors
And they, laughing, take possession of me.
My timid mind is weakened by misfortunes.
My gaze dims with each passing hour.
To die? But there, in the fields beyond,
My husband waits unforgiving.

From the distant shores of the Nile
The seafarer Pausanius[4] brought
To Rome the skins of fallow deer,
Swaths of Egyptian fabrics,
And an enormous crocodile.

It was the time of the insane
Depravations of the Emperor Caracalla.
The god of the merry and carefree
Decorated capricious cliffs
With lines of noisy crowds.

In golden, innocent misfortune,
The sun was sinking into the sea,
And in purple garments
The Emperor has come to the sea
To meet the crocodile.

Bearded wanderers
Bustled by the galley.
And graceful hetaeras[5]
Raised their marble-like fingers
In honor of the goddess Venus.

And like some wondrous tale,
Like a spoiler of peace,
The crocodile glistened by the vessel
With its emerald-colored scales
On a silver pontoon.

---

4   The Greek geographer from the 2nd century AD.
5   Hetaera – a courtesan or mistress, especially in ancient Greece

FROM *A FOREIGN SKY*, 1912

BY THE FIREPLACE

A shadow floated in... The fireplace was burning out,
With his hands across his chest, he stood by himself,

With his gaze fixed far into the distance,
He spoke bitterly about his grief:

"I penetrated the depths of unknown lands,
My caravan has traveled for eighty days;

There were ridges of terrifying mountains, forests,
And sometimes strange towns in the distance.

More than once, in the evening stillness,
A faint howl reached our camp.

We cut wood, we dug trenches,
Lions approached us in the evening.

But there were no cowardly souls among us,
We shot at them, aiming between their eyes.

I dug out an ancient temple from under the sand,
And a river was named after me.

And in the land of lakes, five great tribes
Obeyed me and observed my law.

But now I am weak as though I were gripped by a dream,
My soul is ailing, it is gravely ill.

I have finally come to know fear,
Buried here among four walls;

Even the flash of a rifle, even the splash of a wave
Are not able now to break these chains..."

And, concealing evil triumph in her eyes,
A woman in the corner listened to him.

ABYSSINIAN SONGS

"Abyssinian songs" were Gumilev's variations on the original folksongs that he collected during his travels to Abyssinia. Gumilev did not know the Ethiopian language, so the songs were translated for him into French and he then translated them into Russian. Gumilev claimed that the poems published in A Foreign Sky are his own works based on motifs from Abyssinian folklore, and he intended to publish the originals later.

I. A WAR SONG

A rhinoceros tramples our *durro*,[6]
Monkeys steal away our figs,
But worse than the monkeys and the rhino
Are the marauder Italians.

The first flag was raised flapping over Harar,
This is the city of chief Makonnen.
Afterward, the ancient Aksum arose,
And hyenas began howling in Tigre.[7]

Through the forests, mountains and plateaus
Cruel murderers roam,
You, who slit throats, you
Will drink fresh blood today.

Steal your way from one bush to another
As serpents crawl to their prey,
Leap down swiftly from the cliffs—
Leopards have taught you how to pounce.

---

6   *Durro* – Ethiopian wheat.
7   A province and an ethnic group in Abyssinia.

The one who obtains more rifles in battle,
Who sticks more Italians with a knife
Will be called by his people an *askir*[8]
Of the whitest horse of the *Negus*.[9]

II. FIVE OXEN

Five years I served a rich man,
I guarded his horses in the fields,
And for this, the rich man presented me
With five oxen, trained to the yoke.

A lion killed one of them,
I found its prints in the grass,
I should have guarded the paddock better,
I should have left a fire for the night.

The second ox became rabid,
Stung by a buzzing hornet, and fled
Five days I wandered in thick woods,
But I could not find the ox anywhere.

As for the other two, my neighbor poured
Poisonous henbane into their swill
And they lay on the ground
With their blue tongues sticking out.

I slaughtered the last one myself,
To have something to feast on
At the hour when my neighbor's house was on fire
With the neighbor, all bound-up, screaming inside.

---

8   *Askir* – a soldier, a warrior.
9   *Negus* is the Ethiopian king

III. THE SLAVES' SONG

In the morning when birds awake,
When gazelles run out into the fields,
A European comes out of his tent,
Snapping his long whip.

He sits down in the shade of a palm tree
Wrapping his face with a mosquito net,
He places a bottle of whiskey next to himself
And whips the slaves whom he thinks are too lazy.

We must clean his clothes,
We must guard his mules
In the evening we eat salted meat
That went bad in the morning.

Long live our European master!
He has such long-range rifles,
He has such a sharp saber,
And his whip lashes so painfully.

Long live our European master!
He is brave, but so slow-witted,
He has such a delicate body,
It will be sweet to plunge a knife into it.

IV. THE WOMEN OF ZANZIBAR

Once a poor Abyssinian heard
That far to the north, in Cairo,
The women of Zanzibar dance
And sell their love for money.

Long ago he became bored

With the fat women of Habesh,[10]
With the sly and evil women of Somali,
And with the dirty day laborers from Kaffa.[11]

And the poor Abyssinian set out
Riding his only mule
Over mountains, steppes and forests
Far, far to the north.

Thieves attacked him,
He killed four and escaped,
And in the Senaar's thick forests
Hermit elephants trampled his mule.

Twenty times new moons had risen
Before he reached the gates of Cairo
He remembered then that he had no money,
And went back along the same road by which he had come.

---

10   A province in northern Abyssinia
11   An ancient kingdom conquered by Menelik II in 1887

FROM *THE QUIVER*, 1915

AN AFRICAN NIGHT

Midnight fell, impenetrable darkness,
Only the river shines in the moonlight,
And beyond the river an unknown tribe,
Lighting campfires, makes a commotion.

Tomorrow we'll meet and find out
Who'll be ruler of this place,
They're aided by the spirit of the black stone,
The golden cross on our neck helps us.

I again make the rounds between pits and mounds
Supplies will be here, the mules over there;
In this gloomy land of Sidamo[12]
Even the trees fail to grow tall.

I have a cheerful thought that if we prevail,
As we've already prevailed over so many,
Like a yellow serpent, the road
Will again lead us from hill to hill.

If tomorrow the waves of the river Uabe
Swallow my death-sigh in their roar,
In the pale sky I'll see, while dying,
The black god doing battle with the fiery one.

Eastern Africa, 1913

---

12   The Southwestern part of Abyssinia

FROM *THE BONFIRE*, 1918

THE AZBAKIYA

How strange—exactly ten years have passed
Since I've seen the Azbekiya,
A huge Cairo garden, that evening
Solemnly illuminated by the full moon.

I was tormented by a woman at that time,
And neither fresh and salty sea breeze
Nor the din of exotic markets,
Nothing could console me.
I prayed to God for death,
And prepared to hasten it myself.

But this garden resembled in every way
The sacred groves of the young world:
Three slender palm trees raised their branches
Like young maidens to whom God descended;
And on the hills, like wise druids,
Majestic plantain trees crowded together,

In the darkness a waterfall shone white,
Resembling a rearing unicorn;
Night butterflies were flying
Among flowers that rose so tall,
Or perhaps among the stars that were so low to the earth
They resembled ripened barberries.

And I remember I exclaimed "Life is loftier
Than grief, more profound than death itself! Receive, O Lord,
My vow, given of my own free will; regardless of
What will happen and what grief and humiliation
Will be my lot, I will not think
About an easy death before
I once again step on a similar moonlit night
Beneath the palms and plantain trees of Azbakiya."

How strange—exactly ten years have passed,
And I cannot think of the palm trees,
Plantains, or the waterfall that
Shone white in the darkness like a unicorn.
I'm startled and look around when I hear
In the droning wind or in the sound of voices from afar,
In the terrifying silence of the night
The word full of mystery: Azbakiya.

Yes, only ten years have passed, but I, a somber wanderer,
Must go back again, I must see
The seas, the clouds, and foreign faces,
Everything that no longer interests me.
I have to once again enter that garden and repeat
My vow or say I have fulfilled it
And now I am free . . .

THE TENT, 1921

INTRODUCTION

Deafened by the roar and clatter,
Decked in flames and smoke,
It is of you, my Africa, that whispering
Seraphim speak in the heavens.

When they open your Gospels,
The tale of your terrible and wonderful life,
They are thinking of the untested angel
Who's appointed to look after you, reckless one.

Listen to this tale of your deeds,
Fantasies, and the animal soul.
You are hanging on the ancient tree of Eurasia
Like an enormous pear.

Destined to you, I will speak
Of chiefs decked in leopard skins
Who in the darkness of forests
Lead fearsome warriors to victory;

Of villages with ancient idols
That smile unfriendly smiles;
Of lions that stand over villages
Swatting their ribs with their tails.

Grant me for this a smooth road,
Where there is no path for a common man,
Let them name with my name
A still undiscovered black river;

Grant me also a last favor with which
I will leave for the heavenly realm:

Let me die under the sycamore
Under which Mary rested with Jesus.

THE RED SEA

Greetings, Red Sea, a soup of sharks,
A bath of Negroes, a cauldron of sand!
Instead of moist moss, limestone blooms
Like stone cacti on your cliffs.

On your islands, in scorching sand,
Left by the tide that grows at night,
Sea monsters die in anguish:
Octopi, tritons, and swordfish.

Hundreds of dugouts from the African shore
Move into the sea in search of pearls;
And hundreds of feluccas from the Arabian shore
Try to drive them back to the East.

If they catch a Negro, he'll be led,
To the slave market at Hodeida[13] in chains,
But an unfortunate Arab often finds rest
In your hot, muddy, red waves.

Like a teacher among naughty children,
An ocean liner sometimes passes through the dugouts
Behind its propeller, water seethes like a blizzard,
On its deck are red roses and ice.

You are powerless before it; let the hurricane roar;
Let waves rise like crystal mountain ridges.
The captain will light a cigarette and sigh:
"Thank God it cooled down! I'm sick of this heat."

---

13   A city in western Yemen on the Red Sea.

For the whole day, like a swarm of dragonflies,
Golden flying fish are seen over your waters.
By sand dunes bent like a scythe,
Shoals, just like flowers, are red and green.

The air is shining, filled with a translucent fire,
The sun, like a fabulous bird, looks from above:
"Red Sea, you are regal in daytime,
But at night you are twice as brilliant!"

As soon as water vapors glide into the sky like a cloud,
Shadows of black mermaids will glisten in your waves,
The alien constellations—crosses and axes
Will light up above you in the heavenly gardens.

Your bewitching currents begin
To flicker like sparkling Bengal lights,
There are sparks and rays in them as though,
Envious of the sky, you want to create your own stars.

When the moon floats up to its zenith,
The wind rushes by, bringing the scents of the forest,
From the Suez to the Bab-el-Mandeb[14]
Your surface resonates like the lyre of Eolus.[15]

From the forested gorges elephants approach your slopes,
Carefully listening to the noise of the tidal waves,
To worship the reflection of the waning moon,
They approach the water and fear the sharks.

Do you remember how you were the only sea
That once fulfilled God's behest,
You tore apart the seams of your surf
So that Moses could pass and the Pharaoh would die.

---

14 The strait between Arabia and northeast Africa.
15 One of two brother gods of the wind, whose lyre touched by the wind played beautiful music.

EGYPT

You are a picture from an ancient book
That has delighted my nights
With these emerald plains
And the fans of sprawling palms.

Canals, canals, and more canals
Rush past along walls of clay,
Irrigating the cliffs of the Damietta[16]
With rose colored splashes of foam.

And these ridiculous camels,
With bodies of fish and the heads of birds,
Walk like huge ancient wonders
From the depths of luxuriant, colorful seas.

That is how you will see Egypt
At that thrice-divine time when
The human day is drunk up by the sun
And, bewitching, water billows.

To the distant blooming platans
You come as a wise man who
Before came to speak to the Eternal One,
Loving birds and stars forever.

Is this water lapping peacefully
Between heavy mill wheels,
Or is it the snow-white Apis lowing
Bloodied by a chain of roses?

Is this the gaze of the gracious Isis
Or a glimmer of the rising moon?

---

16   A city and area in the Nile Delta on the Mediterranean Sea, not far from Alexandria

Come to your senses! The pyramids,
Terrifying and dark, rise up before you.

On their ledges gray from the moss
Eagles land for nocturnal rest,
While deep inside, corpses are at rest
Unfamiliar with decay, enveloped in darkness.

The sphinx has sprawled guarding the shrine,
Looking and smiling from on high.
It awaits guests from the desert
Of whom you know nothing yet.

But the single master of Egypt,
The flood of the Nile, is lapping
Over the chambers of Elephantine
And the gardens of Memphis and Phoebes.

There, looking at the deserted river
You'll exclaim: "But this is a dream!
I am not chained to our age
If I see through the abyss of time.

Wasn't it in my presence,
Carrying out the pharaoh's wishes,
That naked slaves from the desert dragged stones
And erected these pillars?

Wasn't it in my presence, centuries later,
That choruses of dancing priestesses
Sang hymns in honor of the crocodile
And prostrated themselves before the Ibis?

And languishing for her dear Anthony,
Lifting up her beautiful eyes
Over the Nile, Cleopatra counted
Sails that passed by her."

But enough! Is it really your wish
To always live among the delights of the past?
Don't you rejoice at today's night,
Don't the greens of today please you?

It's not a remnant of an ancient crypt
Under your foot that taps on the stones,
Egypt possesses a different soul
And another solemn festiveness.

Like the wondrous Fata-Morgana,[17]
A city appears, a captive of night,
Over the mosque of sultan Hassan,
A minaret pierces the moon.

On cool, open terraces women
Brush the gold of their hair,
And treat their dark-eyed girlfriends
To rose-jelly and ginger.

Sheiks pray, looking stern and imposing,
The Koran lies open before them
Where Persian book miniatures
Appear like butterflies from fabulous lands.

Lounging on cozy, plush sofas,
Before a hookah and fiery coffee
Poets are reciting their verses
At night in cool coffee shops.

Not for nothing the country had coined
A saying that is known all over the world:
"Who has tasted the water of the Nile
Will forever want to return to Cairo."

---

17   A mirage associated with the legendary enchantress Morgan le Fey of Arthurian Romance.

It doesn't matter that the British are the masters,
They drink their wine and play football,
And that the sacred absolute rule of Hediv
Lost his power in the High Divan.[3]

Let it be! But the true king of the country
Is not an Arab, not a white, but the one
Who leads black buffalos
With the plow and the harrow into the field.

Although he lives in a house of silt,
He dies like a beast in the woods,
He is the favorite of the sacred Nile
And the fellah is his contemporary.

It is for him that the annual deluges
Of this reddish, tousled water
Flood these rich grain fields
Where the harvest is collected three times each year.

It is he who is protected by the rapids
With a band of sharp-edged stones
From an unexpected, midnight signal of danger.
From short-tipped Nubian swords.

The sleepless kite knows for certain
That the entire country is just this river
Lined by a small green border
And by another golden one, made out of sand.

If a pensive stork settles
Near to your fields,
Write a note in English
And tie it to its wing.

---

[3] The Turkish Council of State

In the spring when the stork
Returns, you'll receive a greeting
From Egypt, from the merry fellah children
Written on a eucalyptus leaf.

THE SAHARA

All deserts are kindred to one another,
But Arabia, Syria, the Gobi
Are just the lulling of the Sahara's wave
That is rising in satanic spite.

The Red Sea and the Persian Gulf splash,
Very deep is the snow in the Pamir Mountains,
But the deluge of the Sahara's sandy ocean
Reaches as far as green Siberia.

Neither in the coolness of forests,
Nor in the expanse of the sea, but only in this desert
Will you not want people and will meet no one,
You will love only the wind and the sun.

The sun lowers its face from the blue height
And it is as young as a virgin's face.
Like streams of the overflowing sun,
Golden sand dunes are remarkably smooth.

There are towers, palaces of porphyry cliffs
Everywhere, fountains and palms standing on guard,
The sun on the smooth surface of airy mirrors
Paints a radiant mirage with its brush.

In the autumn, this heavenly painter
Spreads out lilac shadows
By the foot of the mountains and plants,
On the sand, as though on a smooth, golden board.

Once the heavenly singer, the sun, gives a sign,
Harmonious chimes will resound—
This is limestone, filled with fire,
Bursting out and scattering as the red dust.

Cliffs shine, the stony beds of ancient rivers
Grow dark beneath them far below.
You will say that the Sahara looks like
A sea in a storm raging with waves.

Look closer: this eternal glory of sand
Is only a reflection of this celestial fire.
The Sahara looks like the sky where
Light clouds sleep and rainbows meander.

The violent wind in the desert is
Its second master. It rushes in spurts
Like a precious Eastern strider
Through tall mounds and spacious plains.

In its presence, the sand rings and sings, rising up,
It recognizes its master.
The air grows dark, the sun's pupil begins
To look like the core of a pomegranate.

Like monstrous trunks of palm trees,
Whirlwinds of dust, swelling, fly up,
They curve and, swaying, pass in the darkness,
You secretly think they will never collapse.

With their heads disappearing in clouds,
These terrible flying gray serpents
Will wander to the end of ages,
More threatening with every hour.

But a moment... and one falls behind and shudders,
And the sand pile subsides.

This means it has stumbled on its way
Into a fearfully bleating camel.

When on the cleared surface of plains
All of them will lie down like new mountains,
The *khamsin*[19] will leave for the Mediterranean Sea
To intoxicate blood and to sow seeds of discord.

A caravan stops, and its guide
Probes everywhere with his staff in alarm,
A familiar spring splashes about somewhere close,
But the caravan doesn't know the way to it now.

In oases you can hear the neighing of horses,
And one smells the aromatic spikenard flowering beneath palms,
Although these islands are rare in an ocean of fire
Like spots on a cheetah's skin.

Here the deafening noise of battle often resounds,
Spears shine, burnooses flutter.
Tuaregues who rule over the western land
Are disliked by the Thebeans in the east.

While they fight over a palm forest,
A camel, or a slave woman's smile,
Their native Tibesti, Murzurk, Gadames[20]
Are covered by sand from the desert.

This happens because desert winds are proud,
And they don't know the limit of willfulness.
They knock down walls, cover over gardens
And fill ponds with fine white salt.

Perhaps, only a few centuries are left

---

19 A hot Southern or Southeastern wind in Egypt that blows for about 50 days in March, April, and May.
20 Mountain areas and oases on the northern Saharan border

Before the sand's ferocious packs
Will attack our ancient, green world,
From the blazing youthful Sahara.

They will fill up the Mediterranean Sea,
Cover Paris, Moscow, and Athens,
We will believe that the celestial fires
Are Bedouins on their camels.

And when, finally, Martian ships
Appear by our planet's globe,
They will see only an ocean of gold
And will give it the name: Sahara.

THE SUEZ CANAL

Flocks of days and nights
Cast spells over me,
But I don't know ones brighter
Than those in the Suez Canal.

Where ships sail
Not in a sea but in puddles,
In the midst of the land
Like a caravan of camels.

Oh, how many birds
Are here on the rocky slopes,

Those blue fables,
Long-legged ones, with large jowls!

You can see lizards
Golden-green
As if they were splashes of the sea
Frozen on the slopes.

While we walk, we toss fruit
To some Arab children
Who sit by the edge of the water,
Playing pirate.

They're shouting
So loud and frolicsome.
And a marabou stork hisses and
Curses as we pass it.
When finally night
Lands like a kite
On the sand, fires will tremble
In front of and behind us;

Some are redder than coral,
Others are green and dark blue—
A water carnival
In the African desert.

The smoke from the Bedouins' campfires,
Carried by a light wind
From distant mountains,
Wafts past us.

From collapsed walls,
By the bend of the canal
A hyena's laughter and
The howling of a jackal can be heard.

Answering them, a passing ship,
Making the nocturnal stars sad,
Sends to sleeping Africa
The melodies of a piano.

SUDAN

Ah, today in the morning
Drums stretched with crocodile skin
Probably sound too loudly—
Sorceresses, too, wail piercingly
On the cliffs of the Nubian Nile,
Because the heart sinks,
The forehead is hot, the eyes have trouble seeing,
And in your dreams there are bustling piers,
The voices of swarthy sailors,
A merry sea in patches of foam,
And beyond the sea is the canyon of Darfur,
Galleries of the forests of Kordofan
And the quiet waters of Bornu.[21]

Cities, on which the sun shines,
Are like treasures in the green overgrowth,
And from them, like threatening hands,
Minarets rise to the sky.
On thrones of ivory,
Kings and rulers of Sudan
Sit stately, like ancient nightmares,
Next to each, a chained lion
Squints its eyes and raises its head,
Licking human blood off its whiskers.
Next to each, a thick-lipped executioner
With shining skin, black
Like the soul of a powerful ruler,
Wearing a red shirt, plays with his poleaxe.

Before them, slave traders
Proudly exhibit their goods,
People moan in heavy shackles,
The whites of their eyes flash in the sun.

---

21 A state and traditional empire in northeastern Niger. The great water is Lake Chad.

Chiefs from the desert ride by,
Long ostrich feathers flutter
Over the heads of prancing horses,
Haughty Frenchmen walk by
Cleanly shaven, all dressed in white.
They have papers with seals in their pockets.
On seeing them, the rulers of Sudan
Rise slowly from their thrones.

All around, on the wide plains
Where the grass hides giraffes,
The Gardener of Almighty God
In the silvery mantle of wings
Created a replica of Eden:
He spread out shady groves
Of fanciful mimosas and acacias,
Planted baobabs on the hills,
In the galleries of cool forests
Where it is light and cool as in a Doric temple,
He etched deep rivers
And in a mighty impulse of joy
He created quiet Lake Chad.

Then he smiled like a boy
Who had thought up an amusing trick,
Gathered here the very fantastic,
Wondrous animals and birds.
Borrowing colors from the desert sunsets,
He painted feathers of parrots,
Gave two tusks to the elephants, which
Are whiter than clouds of the African sky,
Dressed the lion in golden garments
And the leopard—in one with colorful spots,
For the rhinoceros he made the horn the color of amber
And gave the gazelle the eyes of a maiden.

After that he left for the distant stars
Perhaps, to paint them too.
Animals roam as God prescribed them to do,
Gathering at a waterhole together.
They don't know that they are fantastically beautiful,
That you cannot find others like them,
Even a hunter does not realize it,
Hiding in the heat of the noon
With his poison-tipped arrow behind a bush.
And then he shouts over the slain beast,
Performing a ritual hunter's dance.
He then carries his precious booty
To the sovereigns of Sudan.

The inhabitants of the savannas sometimes
Are brought together by grass fires.
The day when the sun is eclipsed
With the ashes blown by the wind.
And like an unheard, crimson beast,
Flames stir on the plains,
That day is a deafening feast
Which the hospitable Devil has arranged
For Lady Death and Brother Horror:
On that day, you cannot recognize men
In the swarm of animals that are
Burnt, roaring, striking with fangs
And horns, and understanding just one thing: fire!

Evening. Your eyes cannot distinguish
The bright threads in the white belt;
This is the sign that Muslims
Must perform ablutions before Allah,
Some who live in the woods by a river with water,
Others living in the waterless desert with sand.
People pray from the bare sand slopes
Of the restless Red Sea
To the green, foamy
Waves of the Atlantic.

It is quiet in Sudan, and
Above it, above that giant child,
I truly believe, God is looking down.

ABYSSINIA

Between the shore of the stormy Red Sea
And Sudan's mysterious forest, one can see
A country that looks like a lioness at rest
Spread out among four high plateaus.

The north is bottomless, endless marshes.
Black snakes stand on guard around them,
There the ominous yellow-faced flock
Of their sisters-fevers has found a shelter.

Somber mountains frown above them.
Those are the Tigré, the age-old abode of brigandage
Where chasms bare their teeth, and forests are tangled,
Mountain peaks stand covered with snowy silver.

In the fruit-bearing Amhara, people sow and reap,
Zebras like to blend into domestic herds of cattle.
And in the evening, a chilly wind carries out
Sounds of guttural songs and the rumble of strings.

An Abyssinian sings, his *bagana*[22] is weeping,
Resurrecting the past that is full of charms.
There was a time when the royal capital
Gondar rose before Lake Tana.

Under the platans, a scholar discussed the existence of God,
Captivating the crowd with melodious verse,

---

22   A stringed musical instrument.

Artists painted King Solomon
Between the Queen of Sheba and a good-hearted lion.

But believing Shoa's refined sweet talk,
Abyssinia's wise elephant, the Negus Negesti,
Moved his throne to the rocky Shoa
From the ancient homeland of poets and roses.

In Shoa, the warriors are cunning, cruel and crude,
They smoke pipes and drink intoxicating *tedj*[23]
They like to listen to drums and war pipes,
To grease their rifles and sharpen the swords.

They conquered for their Emperor Menelik
The Hararites, the Gallas, the Somalis, the Danakils,
The cannibals, and pygmies in the thick forests,
And covered the floor of his palace with lion's furs.

Looking at streams by the foot of the mountains,
At oaks and the celebration of the noon sun's rays.
A European wonders how strangely closely
The people and their land resemble one other.

II

A magical land! You're suffocating at the bottom
Of a hollow basin, the fire flows from above,
Over you a hawk's scream resounds,
But will you notice the hawk in this brilliance?

Palms, cacti, grasses as tall as a man,
Too much of this burnt grass here...
Be careful! Boa constrictors lurk in it,
Panthers and red-haired lions are hiding there too.

Climb up the slopes of the precipices and steep cliffs
Along a treacherous road, and you'll suddenly see

---

[23]   An alcoholic drink

Sycamores and roses all around, merry villages
And a green meadow speckled with people.

There a sorcerer performs a typical miracle,
A snake dances obedient to the tune,
A judge sitting on a stone in the shade hears a case
Of swindling a hundred *thalers* for a sick camel.

Climb higher! How cool the air is!
Fields are empty as in late autumn,
Creeks freeze over at dawn, and the herd
Crowds together under the roof of a dwelling.

Baboons snarl in thickets of spurge;
Dirtying themselves in the sticky, white juice,
Riders gallop, tossing long spears
And shooting the rifles at full gallop.

Only the cliffs are higher, bare rapids precipices,
Where winds migrate and eagles exult,
Man has not climbed up there, and white from the snow
Are the peaks beneath the tropical sun.

Everywhere, above and below, caravans
Breathe in the sun and drink in the unbound expanse,
When they go to the still unexplored terrain,
Searching for elephant tusks and the mountains' gold ore.

I, myself, loved to wander along those roads,
To watch stars in the evening, the size of huge beans,
To run up the hills after the long-horned goats,
To bury myself for the night in the graying moss.

There is a museum of ethnography in the city
By the Neva[24], that is wide and deep like the Nile,

---

24   The Neva River is in the delta on which St. Petersburg is situated.

At an hour when I'll be tired of being only a poet,
I'll long for nothing more than going there.

I go there to touch the savages' possessions
That some time ago I had brought from afar,
To smell their scent, strange, precious, and foreboding,
The scent of incense, roses, and animal pelts.

And I see the sultry sun blazing,
A leopard steals up to its enemy, arching its back,
And my old servant awaits me,
For an enjoyable hunt, in a hut full of smoke.

THE GALLA

For eight days, I led my caravan from Harar
Through the wild mountains of Chercher.
Shooting at gray apes in the trees,
Sleeping among the roots of sycamores.

On the ninth night, I saw from a hill—
I will never forget that moment—
On a distant, barely visible plain
Campfires, like red sparks, glowed all over.

They rushed after one another,
Like storm clouds in the shining blue sky,
Thrice sacred are the nights and strange the days
On the wide, open flatlands of the Galla.

Everything I approached there
Was larger than I had previously seen.
I watched giant women tend to
Huge camels by wide ponds;

And enormous Gallas galloping
Wearing lion and leopard skins
Slashing running ostriches straight from the shoulder
Riding huge, hot-tempered steeds;

How antediluvian men give steamy white milk
To old, dying snakes to drink...
Lowing buffaloes ran away from me
Because they had never seen a white man.

By the entrance to caves at times
I heard the sound of songs and the beating of drums,
Then it seemed to me that I'm Gulliver
Left behind in the land of the giants.

I saw the tall city of Sheikh-Hussein—
The mysterious city, the tropical Rome.
I bowed to the minaret and the sacred palm trees,
I was admitted before the eyes of the prophet.

A fat Negro sat on Persian rugs
In a murky, dirty reception room,
Like an idol, wearing bracelets, earrings, and rings,
Only his eyes shined brilliantly.

I bowed, he smiled at me in response,
Tenderly slapping me on the shoulder,
I presented him with a Belgian handgun
And a portrait of my sovereign.

He kept asking me whether people know
Much about him in distant, barbarous Russia...
As far away as the sea he is famous for his magic,
And his deeds are quite noble:

If you cannot find a mule in the forest,
Or your restless slave runs away,

You'll receive everything back if you promise
To bring Sheikh-Hussein an appropriate gift.

THE SOMALI PENINSULA

I remember the night and a country of sands
And the moon so low in the night sky,

I remember I could not take my eyes
From the moon's golden arc.

There is light and, perhaps, birds sing there,
Flowers bloom over ponds,

There you cannot hear ferocious lions roam,
Filling ravines with their roar,

There mimosas with prickly hands don't grasp
A passer-by on his way to the abyss of the night,

That evening as soon as shadows of bushes began to crawl,
The Somalis began to approach me.

Their chief with a red hat and shaggy hair
Pronounced a death sentence to me.

His derisive gaze from under lowered eyelids
Saw how few people were with me.

Tomorrow is a battle, a merciless, deadly fight
With the howling black mob.

Beneath the camels' feet is the interlacing of bodies,
A downpour of poisonous arrows and spears...
I painfully thought that there on the moon
The enemy wouldn't be able to sneak up on me.

Right at midnight I woke up my caravan,
An ocean rumbled behind the hill.

People were dying in the watery depths, we on the land
Also awaited our end in the dark.

We set off. Grasses breathed
Like the pelt of a sweat-covered lion,

Among sacred black stones, heaps
Of skulls, and bones shone white.

In all of Africa, there is no one more ferocious than the Somalis,
Or a more cheerless land than theirs.

So many white men were pierced by a spear in the dark
Near its sandy wells,

So that Ogaden[25] could speak of their exploits
In the voices of hungry hyenas.

When just before morning the moon set,
It was different: horrifying and red,

I understood that the moon was a knight's shield
That blazes with eternal glory for true heroes.

I ordered that the camels lay down, and entrusted
My freedom-loving soul to my trusty shotgun.

LIBERIA

The shore of the upper Guinea is rich
With honey, gold, and elephant tusks,

---

25   Nomadic Somali tribesmen.

Beyond the fence of the stone ridges,
To a visitor everything is unexpected and new.

In the marshes, lights wander,
A turtle is weightier than a cliff,
Toucans hide in the shadow
Of their own gigantic beaks.

When in the evening, the celestial eye
Submerges into the ocean,
The sails of fishermen from the Cru tribe
Can be seen far away on the horizon.

Each of them is renowned
For being the bravest in facing misfortune,
For being able to save you with one hand
And easily rob you with the other.

During the eighteenth century,
Ships from America used to come
Under full sails
To obtain slaves and ebony.

In the nineteenth century,
The flock of fast-moving steamships
Brought not slaves but free people
Back to the same stone slope.
It seems old biddies from Washington
Understood the character of this land
If the sowing of their moralizing brochures
Bear such plentiful fruits.

Lawyers, masters of the sciences,
Proletarians, pastors, and thieves—
Everyone needed for the republic
Flooded the quiet mountain land.

They settled in . . . The tropical forest,
Submerged in mysterious darkness,
Accepted ladies' hats and men's dinner jackets
Into the multitude of its endless marvels.

"Mr. President, I am your servant,"
Bowing you will quickly say.
Then you'll look up and see that he and
His ministers are blacker than a leather boot.

"Today you are paler than usual,"
Without thinking you'll say to a lady.
You can easily guess
What her answer will be.

Hanging down from thin vines,
Hiding among intricate leaves,
Chimpanzees live in the thick jungle
Near the black city.

From their high perch, in the morning
They listen to Protestants singing in their church,
And they slap their fat bellies as if
Their bellies were big drums.

When at night lights go on,
Listening to evening greetings,
They wander in pairs holding branches
Instead of walking sticks.

One European, offended
By the President, swore
That a large chimpanzee
Had lost his way among city's huts.

He didn't lose nerve, wrapped
His hairy stomach with a patchwork sash

And headed for the President's house—
But the President had gone somewhere.

There, waving his stick, the chimpanzee
Broke dishes like a stumbling drunk.
And for five whole days the chimpanzee
Ruled the country without anyone realizing it.

MADAGASCAR

My heart was beating in mortal languor,
I had wandered the entire day in anguish
At night I dreamt I was sailing
Along a mighty river.

With every moment, the river became
Wider and wider, the light was brighter.
I felt I was in an unknown world
And my boat was weightless.

A red idol on a white stone
Related the answer to the mystery to me,
The red idol on the white stone
Loudly shouted: "Madagascar!"

In litters embellished with gold,
In whimsical carved boats,
On the wide backs of oxen,
And astride loudly neighing horses,

Where thousands of delicate swans
Were singing and quivering,
Throngs of dark-skinned people
Were coming forward one after another.

Humorous plays were composed
About an old suitor coveting
The hand of a beautiful princess
And were staged right on the spot.
Wearing a splendid Hussar uniform,
The most devoted general
Of the Queen of Madagascar
Looked at them with delight.

Among the people, the oxen of Tomatawa,
Looking like piles of black stones,
Devoured delicious grasses
From fields filled with pungent aromas.

I sighed: "Why am I sailing,
Why shouldn't I stay here:
Can it really be that I won't intone
My best poems here?"

Only my voice was not heard
And no one could help me.
Warm night was descending
On the wing of a flying bat.

The heavens and forests grew darker,
The swans fell silent in oblivion . . .
. . . I was lying on my bed
Longing for my wonderful boat.

ZAMBEZI

Like copper in a streak of iron ore,
Fiery sparks are inlaid into the night,
Waves swell out over the Zambezi
And, with whooping, rush away.

Through the frenzy of white lightning
Something can be seen above a wet cliff,
There, a mighty black body
Has leaned on a battleaxe.

You can hear guttural singing.
Certain is the bidding of the Muses
Who are flying around the globe!
He, this Zulu warrior, is singing:

"I was sleeping in an enchanted kraal
And heard a lion's roar,
My heart sank from sweet longing,
My head was swimming.

The sword leapt into my hand,
The door magically flew open,
And a golden, roaring beast
Lay before me, dying.

The spirits of the mist sang to me:
'Let your fury be renowned forever!
You are a worthy descendent of Dingan,[26]
A destroyer, a killer, a lion!'
Since that time, I've always been ready,
I don't feel like sleeping at night,
I need more and more blood
To quench my unquenchable thirst.

Beyond the mountains, as big as clouds,
In the swamps, near a river mouth
I disemboweled Arabs
And slave-traders with my *assagai*.[27]

---

26   Dingan is most likely a reference to Dingane kaSenzangakhona (1795-1840), Zulu chief who became king in 1828.
27   *Assagai* – a sword.

I descended to the Boers in the valley
Carrying to the expanses of the forests
Eight wounds, the beauty of men,
And eleven heads of my foes.

I've been wandering for thirty years,
Afraid neither of people, or fire,
Or gods... but I know what I know:
There is one stronger than I.

This is the elephant in unexplored thickets,
It is, like me, lonely and large.
It plunges its yellowed, broken tusk
Into everyone who passes by.

I dream of it all the time,
I always see it in my dreams
Because the spirits of the mist
Have told me of this elephant-beast.

It is pointless for me to fight with it,
My heart knows I will be killed.
The heavenly chasm will open wide
And my father Dingan will shout:

"Yes, you haven't been a cowardly dog,
You were a lion among fierce lions,
Sit down between me and Shaka
On this bench made of human skulls!"

THE DAMARA

A Hottentot[28] Cosmogeny

It is a sin for a man to be proud,
Human power is paltry:
Some time ago a bird that was
Stronger than man ruled the Earth.

In the early morning, it used to come out
To the steep ocean shores,
Swallowing whole cliffs
And entire islands.

In the sacred evenings
Above high clouds,
It sang, raising its head
To God about divine deeds.

With its feet it drew symbols
That are known in the underworld,
Of everything that was and will be,
It drew them with its feet in the sand.

The bird was so beautiful,
It drew and sang so lively
That this misguided bird
Had decided to compete with God.

God, who designed the world,
Deduced its wicked intentions
And condemned it to suffer,
Rending it into two halves.

---

28   The European emigrants' name for an ethnic group in Southwestern Africa. Khoikhoi is the more common name used for them today.

From the upper part that was singing
To God about divine deeds
The Hottentots were born into the world
Who sing and sing carefree.

From the lower part that drew the symbols
Known in the underworld darkness,
The Bushmen came to live
Who decorate walls with symbols.

Its feathers that flew away
Far into the ocean
Float like white people to this day;
When there will be enough of them,

The former parts will grow together
And will experience happiness again,
The huge, white-feathered bird
Will reign again on Earth.

EQUATORIAL FOREST

I pitched my tent on the rocky slope
Of Abyssinian mountains running to the West
And absent-mindedly watched sunsets
Blazing beneath the green roof of distant forests.

Some birds came flying from there
With emerald feathers and long tails.
At night merry zebras ran out,
I heard their snorting and thumping of hooves.

One day the sunset was especially crimson,
A special fragrance floated from the woods,
A European approached my tent,
He was emaciated, unshaven, and asked me for food.

All night long, he greedily and sloppily ate,
Placing sardines on slices of dried out meat,
Swallowed cubes of *maggi*[29] like medicine pills
And refused to dilute his absinthe with water.

I asked him why he was so deadly pale,
Why his dry hands trembled so much,
Like leaves . . . "It's malaria of the great forest,"
He answered and glanced back in terror.

I asked him about the large open wound
That showed black through the rags on his hollow chest.
What has happened to him? "It was the gorilla of the great forest,"
He answered but did not dare to glance back.

There was a pygmy with him, naked and black, half my size,
It seemed to me that he was a mute.
Like a dog, he sat behind his master
Placing his bulldog face on his knees.

But when my servant jokingly pushed him,
He bared his terrible teeth,
And then for an hour he was agitated and snorted,
Striking the ground with his painted spear.

I provided a bed for my tired guest,
Lied down on the panther's skins but could not sleep.
I avidly listened to the wild lengthy tale,
The feverish raving of the stranger from the woods.

He sighed, "How dark . . . this forest is endless . . .
We won't see sunlight ever again . . .
Pierre, do you still have my diary under your shirt?
This diary is more precious to us than our lives!

---

29   Maggi cubes – powdered seasoning that is used to add flavor to dishes.

Why did the Black people abandon us?
Woe to us, they took our compass . . .
What should we do? Neither beast, nor bird can be seen,
Just whistling and rustling in the treetops and below!

Pierre, do you see the campfires? Someone must be there . . .
Can it be that we are finally saved?
Those are pygmies . . . so many of them gathered together.
Shoot at them, Pierre! Can't you see the human leg on the fire?

Hand-to-hand fighting! Remember that their arrows are poison-tipped!
Hit the one on the stump . . . He's shouting, he's their chief.
Woe to me! My rifle's been blown to pieces . . .
I can't do anything . . . they knocked me off my feet . . .

No, I'm still alive, just tied down . . . you, bastards!
Let me go, I can't watch anymore!
They roast Pierre . . . I played with him in Marseilles,
By the merry sea when we were children.

What do you want from me, you dog? You're kneeling?
I spit at you, repulsive beast!
You're licking my hands? You're tearing off my fetters?
I've understood, you think that I'm your God . . .

Let's flee! Don't take human flesh with us,
Almighty gods do not eat it . . .
Woods, endless woods . . . I'm hungry, Akka,
If you can, catch a big snake!"

He moaned and wheezed, grabbing his chest
And, it seemed, fell asleep by morning.
But when I tried to awaken him,
I saw that flies had crawled over his eyes.

I buried him by the foot of a palm tree,
Placed a cross over a pile of heavy stones

And wrote simple words on a small board:
"A Christian is buried here, pray for his soul."

The pygmy looked indifferent while cleaning his javelin,
But when I had finished my sad ritual,
He jumped up and silently ran down the slope
Like a dear returning to its native woods.

Six months later I was reading French papers.
And my head hung low sadly:
"From the big expedition to the Upper Congo
Still no one has come back."

DAHOMEY

The king said to his commander: "Mighty one,
You are great, like an elephant of the Dahomey forests,
But you are still smaller than the somber heap
Of human heads you had cut off.

Like your valor, skilled warrior,
Your grace knows no bounds.
Do you see the sun above the sea? Go! You are worthy
Of being a servant of my golden father."

Drums began to sound, tambourines started to chime,
Kneeling people howled around,
Amazon women sang drawling, and a trumpet-call
Rolled along the sea from its shore.

The commander bowed to the king and in silence
Jumped from the cliff into the bubbling sea.
He was drowning in the water, but it seemed
It was in the radiance of the setting sun that he drowned.

The drums and shouts were deafening to him,
Splashing salty waves were blinding,
He disappeared. The ruler's face was shining
Like the black sun of the underworld.

THE NIGER

On my map under the unnecessary grid,
Of longitudes and latitudes made for nothing else but to bore us,
I notice something crawling
Like a dropped grapevine, like a long blackened bough.

Around it are cities, like a handful of grapes.
These are Bussa, Gomba, and the king of them, Timbuktu.[30]
The very sound of their names is joyful to me, like the sun,
As the beat of drums, it awakens my dream.

I can't believe, I won't. I'll check in a book.
There should be a limit to people's stupidity.
Yes, it's written—The Niger—Oh, the regal Niger
That's how people dared to insult you!

You flow through Sudan like a solemn sea,
You clash with ferocious packs of sand,
And when you approach the ocean,
One cannot see your shores from your middle.

Pinkish maws of your hippopotami
Are like the piles of an invisible wondrous bridge,
And your crocodiles break ship's propellers
With mighty blows of their tails.

Oh, my Niger, I am preparing another, fantastic
Map, a delight for the eyes,

---

30   Cities on the Niger River.

I will place gold brocade in a wide band
Right on the smooth green satin.

Blood-red rubies will be placed on the left below,
This is a place of strange metallic gods.
Who has buried them in the gloomy ravines of Benin
Among elephant tusks and human skulls?

Further to the right, at the thick groves of Sokoto,[31]
I will place a large emerald on this atlas.
There, hunts are plentiful and the villages are rich,
There, free people sing like birds.

Further, a pale opal, flickering capriciously
With crimson and blue fire hidden in it,
It will remind me sweetly of the valleys of Songhai[32]
And the clay palace of Songhai's sultan.

I will certainly use a marvelous pearl to mark
Timbuktu, the city of shining roofs,
Above which a kite-bird screeches, perplexed,
Seeing mimosas in bloom in the heart of the desert,

Seeing swarthy young women, lithe as grapevines,
Whose breath is more intoxicating than balsamic resins.
Seeing fountains in gardens and blood-red roses
That crown the leaders of schools of poetry.

Africa's heart is full of song and passion,
And I know that if at times we see
A dream for which we cannot find a name,
It is brought by your wind, Africa!

---

31 A river in northwestern Niger.
32 The area in the middle reaches of the Niger River.

FROM *THE PILLAR OF FIRE*, 1921

A LEOPARD

> *If a hunter doesn't burn the whiskers of a killed leopard right away, its spirit will haunt him.*
> An Abyssinian superstition.

In the quiet of the dead of night,
A leopard killed by me
Is busy casting spells
And conjuring in my room.

People enter and leave,
The last one to leave—she
For whom golden darkness
Roams in my veins.

It's late. Mice are beginning to squeak,
The house spirit made a hollow grunt,
And the leopard killed by me
Purrs menacingly near my bed.

"Through the gorges of Debre Berhan[33]
A dove-colored mist floats,
The sun, red as a wound,
Illuminates the place.

The scent of honey and verbena
Is driven to the east by the wind,
And hyenas howl and howl,
Burying their noses in the sand.

My brother, do you hear the howling?
Do you smell the scent, do you see the smoke?

---

33   A city located in central Ethiopia.

For what reason then do you breathe
This sickly humid air?

No, you, my killer, must
Die here in my land
In order for me to be reborn
In my family of leopards."

Can it be that I will be forced to listen to
the cunning call till sunrise?
Why didn't I listen to what they told me,
Why didn't I burn its whiskers?

Now it's too late! An evil power
Has overcome me and come so close:
It has pressed my head
As though it were a bronze hand...

Palm trees... from the sky, a terrifying flame
Burns the sandy reservoir...
A Danakile lies in wait behind a rock
With a flaming spear in his hand.

He doesn't know and will not ask
For the reason of my soul's pride,
He will simply fling that soul
To a place he himself doesn't know.

I cannot fight it any more,
I am calm and I rise,
I will end my life, I know,
By the giraffes' watering hole.

FROM UNCOLLECTED WORKS

<AN ACROSTIC[34]>

Addis Ababa, city of roses.
Near the shores of translucent streams,
Next to the widest of dark canyons
A *div*[35] of the heavens has brought you, diamond city.

Armida's garden...[36] A pilgrim there
Keeps the vow of a cryptic love,
Making us all bow before it,
And the roses are so suffocating, so crimson.

There someone gazes into your soul, full
Of poison and deceit,
Vanishing in groves of tall sycamores
And in the garden paths of murky plantain trees.

1911

I look at Your dress that is as blue
As the Abyssinian sky
And I adorn your album
With my words.

---

34   The initial letters of each line spell the name of Gumilev's first wife and the great Russian poet Anna Akhmatova.
35   A div is a spirit capable of performing magic in Islamic folklore.
36   Armida was a sorceress who enticed knights searching for the Holy Grail to her castle surrounded by an enchanted garden.

<Acrostic>

May one see in this picture
An angel, the sun, and Lake Chad,
Raucous Negroes dressed in nothing but capes,
Young sisters perched in a charabanc,
Sitting slender, graceful as blades of grass.

And the heart rises above all that,
Lanced twice with a ferocious love,
But the heart opened the door for pain and song:
Unfortunately I cannot forget
My thoughts of the man of another faith.

A POEM TO THE MUSIC OF DAVYDOV

I am a dancer from the shores of the Nile,
I am to dance on the scorching sand,
Oh, why have I fallen in love with you,
But I did not see you in love with me.

Evening is near; the sail is being lowered;
In the heady air of myrrh and lemon balm
I stringed glass beads onto my braids
And reclined on the leopard skin.

But, like the waves of the silent Nile,
You wander around sleepy and cold...
Oh, why have I fallen in love with you,
But I did not see you in love with me.

21 June 1911

Palm trees, three elephants, and two giraffes,
An ostrich, a rhinoceros, and a leopard:
Distant mysterious Kaffa,
Once again I am your guest and bard!

Let her, dressed in a light blue dress,
Pass, austere, into the sunset!
Let her not look back at me!
She will wait for bright paradise as before.

CHRISTMAS IN ABYSSINIA

The crescent moon has risen; it's time to go hunting
I told my servant: "The time has come!
Tonight we should track down
A beaver by the swamp."

But grinning in response,
And barely managing to hide his triumph,
He exclaimed: "What are you saying, Gatta,[37]
Tomorrow will be Christmas.

And tonight all animals –
Lions, elephants, and the smallest ones –
They will all come to the gates of heaven
To delight Christ.

And no one of them will be
The first to attack another.
Will not bite or sting,
Will not kick, will not butt.

And when unrecognized by people,
Radiant God will step out into the field,

---

[37]   The Ethiopian form of address to Europeans, an equivalent to "Mister."

They, all roaring, barking, and lowing,
Will crowd by his feet.

If you weren't blind, you could
Also see your beaver there,

But if you hunt it,
You would not see as much good."

I answered: "It's time to sleep!"

1911

ALGIERS AND TUNIS

The Algiers that tore itself
From ancient Europe
Is orphaned in sultry Africa
Like an innocent outcast.

And the sad brother of Algiers,
Tunis, stretches its melancholy cape,
Bent strangely upward,
Toward Italy in the distance.

Here the Romans built buildings,
And the colonnades of the palaces
Are as strong as before
Under the pressure of winds.

By the steep shores,
On green meadows,
Lime and ash-trees are the same
As on the other coast.

And Atlas' mass
Is heavy and black,
As if the Sierra-Nevada
Were kindred to it for ages.

We were afraid of
These steep rocky slopes
When the ships of barbarian pirates
Nested in that place.

Here the waters were bloodied,
Where Cervantes prayed
To the burning sky
For longed-for freedom.

But the days of the Algerian Bey[38]
Have passed since long ago.
After Algiers, Tunis,
Weakened, was subdued.

And having remembered
Former alliances with this region,
The French have occupied
Their hereditary land.

Now these valleys,
The abode of games and songs,
Won't be able to push the Christians
Off the Constantine cliffs.[39]

The crooked knife of the Janissary
Won't cut off their heads,
And from the bullet of Gerard[40]
The last of the lions fell dead.

---

38   A Turkish title for a chieftan.
39   The city of Constantine in Algeria built atop steep cliffs.
40   Jules Gerard (1817-1864) was a famous lion hunter.

In the country turned
Into a magical garden,
The grapes, forbidden till now,
Have blossomed once again.

Cities rose
Among corn fields
Where the French savor
The combination of absinthe and ice.

Respecting the guests,
Bedouins look
At foreign sweets
In large shop-windows.

But even now the South
Has bared its fangs to the North.
The rusty pack of the sands
Keeps crawling out of the desert.

Graves instead of huts there,
Moats instead of lakes...
And the Kabyls[41] retreat,
Snarling back like lions.

But the white man is happy
To fight any foe:
He digs wells,
Plants palms around them.

He comes out to meet
This dry cloud of gold,
Like a knight going to battle
With a colossal dragon.

---

41   A nomadic tribe of Berbers in northern Africa.

And, like the gentle maidens
Of golden old age,
The crops in the quiet fields
Are sustained by no one but him.

<1918-1921>

ABYSSINIAN SONGS

I welcome the Virgin Mary,
She was created pure and merciful
Like a turtle dove.

* * *

One cannot escape death: there once was an Emperor Aba-Danya,[42]
But the leopard's eyes hurt,
He ventures not from his lair.

If only Aba-Danya's horse would not become frightened!
A cowardly horse fears a shadow,
Anything from an elephant to a giraffe.

Whom has he conferred to hold up his shield?
It stills threatens them,
But the people hold it up only out of habit.

And you, Yagatto Makonnen,[43] where are you now?
The silk baggy trousers and the silk sunshade

---

42   The name of Menelik's horse. Horses often became the nickname for their owner in Ethiopia.
43   Prince Makonnen, the governor of Harar, who was second in line to the throne of the Emperor of Ethiopia.

Have been given only to the Negus of Harar.[44]
But even he has fallen asleep forever in Kulubi.[45]

* * *

This night I saw a cat in my dream
Giving birth to kittens.

But I have been told truthfully, without lies,
That all who live will die.

"When your unfortunate hour arrives,
How will you spend it?" I was asked.

Till now I knew nothing unpleasant,
But what will come later – I do not know.

During the day and at night – my thoughts are my friends.

* * *

Menelik said: "I love those who saddle
Mules and horses in order to follow me
And I love those who stay behind in my home.
Let them live as Abraham once lived,
I do not want them to die."

Abraham was a good man
Who spent five hundred years in his tent.
Long live our Negus, as Abraham used to live!
After all, even animals love their elder.

Hararites, Hamgars, Arabs,
Somalis, Gallas, Shangalis –
All were gathered together by the power of our father Menelik.

---

44   The Emperor of Ethiopia Haile Selassie.
45   A small town south of Dire Dawa in eastern Ethiopia.

* * *

The attacking warrior is as strong as a pillar,
He pierces men with his spear as if he were stringing beads.
When he starts off on his horse, cowards run away.
No one can argue with him, he is like a mountain.
Everything a man can gather, he has already gathered,
Because what is lower than the sky and higher than the earth
Is the judge to everyone – Menelik.
He said: "Do as you are ordered!"
The battle has come, and the order was
For everyone to stand by the Emperor's sunshade.
But not everyone obeyed the order, some went to the left.
Those were Tafasa Abaynech and Gibaia Gora.
Enemies pressed on against us,
They made the day a bazaar of blood,
We even forgot our mothers and wives.
Brothers, come as quickly as you can!

* * *

The greatest joy is to watch
People reaping and loading the harvest.
If a horse runs in the road
Or a man walks along it,
Dust rises up.
During a battle the hero is the one
Who deals the very first blow.
I lost my way in the desert and cry and call for help,
There is nothing around me but the heat.
And I am not a common man,
The chief Damoti Berty
Was my father.

This song was sung by me, the Chief of Ulamoses,
Who had killed an elephant and a lion.

* * *

There is fire in the Negus's rifle
And in his harquebus.
Are you silent, prideful woman?
The cane is for a prideful one.

"Yamoti, the chief of Gubba, feed your red horse,"
Father Arrada said.
A black woman for a dark man
Is like an orange cooked in honey.
Balcha[46] sold his land to the people of Deras,
Yagovana is the strongest of all who lived before him.
If you want to love me, we will walk together
Along the direct road to Sidamo.

The river Boroda, we heard, is flooded.
Fitaurari Gaview, we heard, is dead.
I laughed with my teeth, not with my heart,
My soul was cut out from the living me.

Udadji served one communion after another,
But Yagovana has died nevertheless. Farewell, maiden,
You let your hair down below the small of your back,
The part of your hair grows longer and longer.

* * *

As people, upon seeing Liege Iyassu,[47] tremble with fear,
As they shudder, upon seeing Tafari[48] in the distance,
As Ras Makonnen[49] cannot abide women,
As Aba-Mulat keeps his secrets,

---

46   Dejazmach Balcha Safo (1863-1936) was a renowned Ethiopian military commander, who died in the Second Iltalo-Abyssinian War.
47   Heir to the throne.
48   A close relative of the heir. Tafari was the given name of Ras Tafarri Makonnen, the future Emperor of Ethiopia Haile Selassie.
49   Ras Makonnen, Aba-Mulat and Ras Tasama were prominent noblemen

As Ras Tasama loves his secrets,
As Stephanos[50] enjoys cutting off hands,
So eagerly do I want to kill you.[51]

* * *

Hoi, hoi, Aba-Mulat Haile Georgi
Holds court on Thursdays and Fridays,
His servants wear gold necklaces.

The European letter comes by wire
As though in a dream, without a messenger's help.

I am sick with love and I know my enemy:
He leapt from Todoga Malna[52] to Dire Dawa.

"You and I will drink coffee with my fellow countryman,
I am like him, and my rank is equally high,
But a rash does not let me sleep with you."

But even if you were as swift-footed
As the European railroad never tires,
I will always see you in my dreams.

Give me a habit, I want to become a nun!
If I cannot have you
I forsake other men.

---

of the court. Makonnen was governor of Harar province in Ethiopia and the father of Emperor Haile Selassie.

50   The supreme judge. Hands were cut off in Abyssinia as the punishment for thievery.

51   A note in the complete works edition of Gumilev indicates that this expression indicates "the highest tension of sensual love."

52   Two cities in Ethiopia.

* * *

One who kills a lion is greater than one who kills an elephant,
The lion-man cuts off its tail like a tiny bluebell.
In the tall grass of Argaio a lion left tracks and went away,
I despise this idler and, blithely, followed it.

On the high summit of Mt. Abiner it left tracks and went away,
I despise this idler and, blithely, followed it.

The lion bares its fangs, as though it were laughing,
It wags its tail, as though it were shaking a spear,
Now I see it has become enraged.

* * *

Hume and Dagome[53] together own the world-stone,
Djarso and Cole together own the world-stone,
The Chorra do not want peace,
                the Ala do not want to be friends with them.

It is war, my chief, war! My mother could not sleep,
My sister did not remove her sash.

I do not want a chief other than Gabre,
I do not want a stronger chief than Nabro,
For daytime war I do not want anyone else but the strong man Banti.

The angel's son who does not wear even a shirt
Is not supposed to enter the house of the black Hararites.

People who do not dare to scoop water in the river Nazero,
Those who are blind and have no legs, let them go to pick firewood.

A coward is the first to depart for the mountains,
A shameful man climbs a tree.

---

53   These are the names of Galla and Hararite tribes.

But the strong man breaks heads like gourds,
His mother knows how to give birth.

Daytime war is a war with talk;
The Somali Roble was very strong,
                and Roble's mother is a Somali woman,
Who very bitterly cries at dawn.

Earth does not drink the blood of Muslims, you should not spill it;
When I throw my spear, I hit the target, if I go to war, I am not afraid.

* * *

Chavello is a beautiful place where the reed grows,
I know how my horse Mnogaho can gallop,
I know many pastures on the mountain summits.
The Gurezo is a river without water,
Makanne is like water with milk,
On the other side of the city of Djigjilla[54] there is no water,
But in the many-colored Iliho there are many streams,
I did not drink from them, I kissed them instead.

* * *

---

54   A city that borders the Somali desert.

PROSE WRITINGS

PRINCESS ZARA

"Are you really from the Zogar tribe that lives on Lake Chad?" The old woman asked when her companion entered the strip of moonlight.

Without answering, he threw open the cloth that was hiding his face and chest, and the mighty muscles under the dark bronze skin of the African born Arab were revealed before the old woman. A sacred sign on the forehead, given only to especially important envoys, was also revealed. It calmed down the suspiciousness of the old woman's thoughts.

"Well, fine," the old woman muttered, "I know that people from the Zogar tribe can be trusted. They aren't like our Zanzibar men. Those I wouldn't take to the chambers of Princess Zara. What does the daughter of the great Bey mean to them? For them she'd be the same as the goods they load in their ships for Constantinople. But you showed me an amulet that made my old heartbeat. After all, I'm also from Lake Chad. And besides, your coins ring louder and weigh more than ours, which were filed down without exception by the Jerusalem money lenders."

Her companion didn't utter a word, his face was pale, and it seemed that he was thinking intently about something. They were carefully sneaking along the wall in the courtyard of the Zanzibar palace, which was paved with white flagstones.

Somewhere very close to them, an invisible ocean was seething hazily, and the still air of the tropical night was impregnated with its fresh breath. Moonlight was falling in silver strips on the surface of black reservoirs and was reflected in water droplets frozen on the pink marble steps. Stars were dipping low, very close, and were as deceitful and assuring as the eyes of a girl who has sinned and wants to conceal her disgrace. Why did the inhabitant of wide plains and green jungles, a handsome warrior with a lion-tooth necklace come into this abode of luxury and sin?

The pages in the book of destinies have been tangled long ago, and no one knows in what remarkable way he will come to his ruin.

Finally, a black arch appeared before the travelers, as well as a small door leading to the women's half of the harem. Two customary knocks of the bronze mallet, the flashing pupils of a young Negro girl, and they entered. Inside there was only the dim reddish flame of a lantern, but it still allowed you to see the fabulous richness of Persian rugs that decorated the walls and the floor, the seats made of sandalwood with ivory inlays, carelessly scattered musical instruments, and phrases from the Holy Koran that were inscribed in green enamel on golden shields.

They could sense a slight stagnant smell of musk, Indian perfumes, and the scent of a youthful female body. Princess Zara, all wrapped in silk, was sitting on a wide, low ottoman. It seemed that her motionless lips, as if carved from coral, her excessively thin waist, and her beautiful eyes with their mysteriously sad look, were all created not for love, but for something loftier. Engraved golden bracelets jingled on her arms, bare to the elbow, and a narrow headband supported the luxurious weight of her dark hair. The stately visitor understood that he was not mistaken in coming here.

Bowing, his voice faltering anxiously, he asked the princess to send away the women because only in private could he reveal to her his great secret, the secret that brought him to Zanzibar from the smoky lakes and dangerous dales. Zara didn't answer anything, but the old woman hurried off, conducting a slave girl with her.

"Don't be afraid of anything, my child," she whispered to the princess. "He won't do you any harm. People from the Zogar tribe can be trusted."

And she disappeared, subservient, with a reassuring wink and laughter, and the Negro woman followed her like an obedient dog.

The visitor and Zara were left alone.

"Who are you?" Zara asked quietly, so quietly that one could only guess the beauty of her sonorous voice, "Who are you and why did you come?"

Shuddering, the tall visitor answered her:

"I am from the Zogar tribe, from the great and sacred Lake Chad. I am the chief's youngest son and I am considered the strongest of the strong and the bravest of the brave. More than once, I have defeated the roaring gold-maned lions in nocturnal battles, and ferocious panthers were frightened and hid from me in deep ravines when they heard my steps. Olive-skinned maidens from other tribes often sobbed loudly over the corpses of those who had fallen at my hand. But one day, it was not military drums that thundered over the valley; the people of the Zogar tribe had gathered on a hill, and the great priest inscribed the holy sign of messenger on my forehead, showing me the path to you. Following the flow of the river Shari, I came to the Niam-Niam region, where hideous, stunted people devoured each other and prayed to a god who lives in a black stone. The poisonous mists of Ukereve filled my body with the fire of fever, near Ngezi I survived a battle with a huge snake, and the Nyazi people chased me for forty days over my hills until finally, on my left, the silver snows of Kilimanjaro began to glitter. And eight times the crescent moon became a full moon before I came to Zanzibar.

The tall visitor caught his breath, and Zara was silent, just asking him with her simple and tired gaze:

"For what reason?"

So he continued:

"The Zogar tribe has been faithful to the Prophet, and the Prophet has been gracious and kind to the tribe. He has given it wondrous happiness. The Bright Maiden, Allah's most favorite creation, the joy and glory of the people, lives in our forests. Singular and divine in her nature, she never dies, but sometimes leaves her former shell and appears in another one among the poor settlements of humans, and then the great priest points out where one can seek her. The most honored man of the tribe sets out after her. He reveals her lofty purpose to her and leads her into the kingdom of emerald plains and crimson sunsets. There she lives in happy solitude. One can see her only by chance, and even as she is invisible, we pray to her as to the pledge of the higher virtue which the righteous ones receive in the gardens of Allah. Because only if men are strong and pious, women are beautiful and faithful, then will chaste maidens have wide and snow-white wings, although they are unnoticed by human eyes. Their voice is like the lute of ancient poets, their eyes are transparent like the moisture of the spring that quenched the thirst of the exiled Prophet. They are loftier than houris[55], loftier than angels, they are like souls in the seventh circle of the blissful paradise.

The visitor grew silent again, and Zara did not answer either, only her gaze became mysterious and impenetrable, like those stars that shone for the visitor along his way. However, captivated by his great thoughts, the beautiful Arab noticed nothing and continued.

"You who call yourself Princess Zara, the great priest has acknowledged you now. You are the Bright Maiden of the forests, and I call you to claim your possessions. An impatient, fleet-footed camel of the royal breed, with silken white skin, is awaiting us, tied to a palm tree. We will fly like birds

---

55   Houris are beautiful maidens of paradise in Muslim belief.

over forests and plains; we will cross the foaming river in fast dugouts, until the sacred waters of Lake Chad shine blue before us. On the lake's shore there is a valley that is forbidden for people to visit. There are groves of slender palms with wide leaves and ripened oranges that crowd around silver streams where one can smell irises and intoxicating aloes. The gentle and tender sun does not breathe with the heat there, and its glow merges with the coolness of winds. Bees the color of dark gold land on roses there, roses that are redder than the mantles of ancient kings. Everything there—the sun and the roses and the wind—speak and dream about you. You will settle in a beautiful marble grotto, and the waterfalls, gambol about like horses, will delight your quiet gaze, the golden sand will cover your beautiful legs with kisses, and you will smile at the whimsical shells. And when at sunset a flock of giraffes come to the water hole, you will stroke the silk of their royally rich skin, and, fawning, they will look into your delighted eyes.

"You will live like this until you become bored with the enchantment of joy, and wish, like the evening sun, to leave for new incarnations. Then again, a mighty tribe will gather, called by the drumming of the drums, and again the great priest will point out to the virtuous ones where to find you, the one hiding in a new persona. It has happened more than once and will be repeated again and again, millennium after millennium. But now we must hurry... The opal moon in its inevitable fall has already touched the magnolia forest, soon the youthful sun will rise over the pink ocean. Hurry before the servants of the great Bey awaken. The ringing coins will firmly seal the lips of the old woman shut, but if they do not, then anyone from the Zogar tribe is adept in the art of handling daggers."

The visitor finished and stretched his hands to Zara with hope. It was quiet and sleepy in the harem; just the ocean was rumbling behind the wall and some strange, restless bird was crying sadly. Supple as a lily, Princess Zara slowly rose and fastened her mysterious gaze on the Arab. Her strange words rustled quietly:

"You have spoken well, visitor, but I do not know that of which you spoke. If you like me and want to caress me, I will willingly accede to your desires. You are handsomer than that European, who recently also made his way here to the harem at the cost of his gold. But he did not say anything to me; he just smiled and embraced me. I stood before him like a purchased slave, but the bitterness of his caresses was sweet to me, and I cried when he left. Now you are before me. If you so desire, I will be yours."

And, partly opening the silk fabric on her chest and partly closing her eyes, she waited.

The tall visitor looked at her with a gaze mad from torment. So that is her nature, the Bright Maiden of the forest, whom he had venerated all his life, to whom his fathers and grandfathers had prayed as well! So here she was, humiliated, and unable to recognize her shame, with a sinful smile on her tender lips! Crimson lightning bolts of thought interlaced in his mind; some triumphant monster had stepped right onto his heart with his ugly foot. Wide plains, days of merry hunts, the joys of glory, what did all of this mean before the inhuman suffering that had gripped his soul?! He felt a sharp dagger, sure and firm, strike into his chest. And staggering, the strong warrior fell face down, shuddering and spilling his burning blood onto the expensive Persian carpets.

The supple Zara stood leaning, stock still, against the wall decorated with patterns, and incapable of understanding what had happened. Proud in her beauty, she only had wanted to test if her charm would remain unconquerable even in humiliation. She did not understand to what she had been called. Regret had already begun to stir in her soul; and she did not understand why, following her dangerous and girlish caprice, she had lied and deceived the visitor who had called her to the possibility of unimaginable happiness.

And just before sunset, a ferocious hyena tore apart the snow-white camel that had been tied to a palm tree.

THE FOREST DEVIL

A merry morning wind ran through the dense thicket by the Senegal River, making the grass, still spared by the scorching tropical sun, ripple wildly, and the spotted, graceful giraffes shudder nervously on their way to the water hole. Big golden beetles were buzzing, multicolored butterflies looked like flowers that someone had tossed up high in the air, and content hippos were bellowing, submerging themselves in the mire of coastal marshes. Morning exultation was in full swing when a poisonous black snake, not knowing why exactly, but simply in a fit of momentary hatred, bit a large old baboon, who had long ago left his flock and had been wandering in the woods like a lonely, ferocious vagrant. Madly yapping, he seized a heavy stone, and started chasing the offender, but soon after, stopped, having decided instead to look for the healing grass, which, among the animals, is known only to dogs and their distant relatives, the baboons. He had long known a secluded hollow with such grass and now had no doubt about his salvation, if only the forest creek hadn't flooded and separated him from his desired destination.

In any case, he had to try, and with a malicious growl the baboon set out on his way, limping on his injured paw. At the sound of his steps, small animals hid in their burrows, and fiery flamingoes circled in flocks above the woods, having flown up from the silent blue lakes. Once, even a panther that had stayed out too late pricked up its ears and readily arched its lithe, silken back, but after it had seen whom it had encountered, it graciously jumped up on a tree and pretended that it was going to sleep. No one dared to bother the irritated vagrant of the forest in his swift run, and soon he could see a band of blue water before him through thickly entangled branches. Unfortunately, it wasn't the creek that he used to know, but rather a seething, muddy stream that was carrying broken palms and corpses of animals to the sea, amid foam and splashing.

The baboon's' fears were justified: winter rains had done their work. Still, downstream there was a ford that had never been washed out even by the strongest storms. Understanding that this was his only chance for salvation, the alarmed baboon set off on his way once again. Snake poison acts slowly on animals, and the baboon still only vaguely felt a characteristic urge to writhe and roll on the ground. The bitten leg hurt unbearably, but the desired ford was already nearby. The baboon could already see the cliff that looked like a sleeping buffalo and that pointed to the right direction for him. The baboon hastened his steps but suddenly stopped, shuddering from furious astonishment: the ford was occupied.

Tree trunks had been skillfully laid to make a wide and rather convenient bridge, across which an endless crowd of people and animals was moving. Looking carefully, one could notice that the crowd was divided into orderly groups.

Four rows of elephants, fully covered with bronze and shining copper armor, were followed by a troop of lancers: strong and well-built men carrying gilded shields and spears with golden tips.

Following them, a rhinoceros was walking slowly and ponderously; it was enmeshed in massive silver chains that black slaves pulled on both sides so that it could only move forward. Next was the chief of the party who was prancing on a purebred steed surrounded by a crowd of helpers, most of them young men from rich families, groomed and perfumed. A group of girls and women was traveling under their protection; they were sitting in intricately arranged baskets instead of saddles. Slaves scurried amid carts with tents, food supplies, and luxury items that were at the rear of the procession. Then everything would begin all over again. One troop followed another, and it was difficult to say how many had passed and how many were still hidden in the depth of the forest. All people, except for the slaves, had light golden skin of that noble hue which distinguished the inhabitants of Carthage from the rest of the inhabitants of Africa. The luxurious clothes, the massive amounts of gold and silver, the silk tents, and the captured rhinoceros indicated the richness and nobility of the chief of these troops. Indeed, the beautiful Gannon, Apollo's brother, as he was called by the smooth-tongued Greeks, was the first potentate of Carthage, the city first in fame. Now, accompanied by the entire court, he was traveling to the mysterious Senegal River from whose shores precious stones, wondrous birds, and the best battle elephants had been brought to him and his ancestors from time immemorial.

II

The baboon understood that it was doomed if it waited to the end of the procession, and a furious agitation took over him. Little by little it turned into that wild madness when eyes are clouded with a black shroud, fists are clenched with a terrible power, and teeth themselves find the enemy. While feeling just such a fit rushing through him, the baboon tried to restrain himself, but it was too late.

In a moment, in a mighty leap, he landed on the neck of one of the passing horses that reared and neighed shrilly from sudden terror, and galloped madly into the forest. The girl sitting on it convulsively grabbed it by the mane in order not to fall during this frenzied gallop. She was dressed in red silk clothes and her naked breasts were strapped in a net woven from golden threads, as is custom among wealthy families. Her haughty young face would have been beautiful if not for the unnaturally gaping eyes and pale lips that had turned it into the embodiment of terror. The horse was well-built, luxurious, with blue veins showing through its white skin, and it was obvious that it could flee from any enemy if only that enemy were not sitting on it. The horse's gallop began to grow slower and slower. It stumbled several times and finally, breathing heavily, it fell, with its throat torn apart by the terrible beast. Its riders fell as well. The girl jumped up quickly, but out of terror, she wasn't able to flee and leaned with her back against a tree, resembling the kind of ivory statue that is placed in the temple of the goddess Ishtar. The baboon stood on all fours and yelped hoarsely. His rage was satisfied with the death of the horse, and he already wanted to rush off for the healing grass, but inadvertently taking a look at the girl, he stopped. The baboon recalled a young Negro woman whom he had caught recently alone in the forest and those moans and cries escaping her lips while he shamelessly amused himself with her body.

And an animal-like, keen desire to possess this girl in red clothes and to hear her plea suddenly flared up in the baboon's head; and a light shiver shook his hideous body.

The snake's poison and the urgency to look immediately for the grass were forgotten. Unhurriedly, with the vile foam of desire around his ugly maw, the baboon started to approach his victim, taking pleasure in her terror. Her lips quivered like those of a child who had dreamt a bad dream, but the arched eyebrows frowned with pride, and outstretching her beautiful bare arms with a forbidding gesture, she began to speak quickly and imperiously. She promised the merciless revenge of the goddess Ishtar to the beast approaching her if it only dared to touch her garments, and she spoke also about the mercilessly accurate arrows of great Gannon's servants.

Trees rustled around them, carefree birds cried out, and there was no salvation for her. But the snake's poison was doing its work, and as soon as the baboon grabbed the edge of the silk garment and tore it, he suddenly felt that some insurmountable power had thrown him on the ground, and he convulsively started to writhe, hitting his head against the stones and grabbing at tree trunks. At times, by an incredible exertion of will, the baboon managed to stop his convulsions for a moment, and then he rose on his front paws and turned his unseeing eyes toward the girl with difficulty. But immediately his body shuddered and, laboriously turning his head, he flapped all his limbs in the air.

Shivering, the nearly naked girl looked at the horrific sight. "Ishtar, Ishtar, it is she who has helped me," she whispered, looking around as if afraid of seeing the beautiful but formidable goddess.

When the Carthaginians sent to look for her had arrived, they found her lying unconscious, three steps away from the dead animal.

III

The mighty Gannon was great and handsome. It was to his tent that the girl who had been found was brought to be judged.

Twelve great priests stood on the steps of his portable throne, and forty commanders of troops circled him in rows. The rescued girl appeared before the court of law; she was bound, but as proud as before. Women glanced at her maliciously, young girls averted their gaze, and only smiling children handed her flowers. Gannon himself was quiet and radiant as usual, and he tenderly stroked a small tame monkey that had taken shelter in his lap with his thin, pampered hand. One of the priests arose, shaking the sleeves of his chlamys[56] embroidered with stars and secret signs, and began his oration: "O beautiful Gannon, beloved of the gods; you, the priests of Ammon and Ishtar; and you, the famous people of Carthage, you all know that today a forest devil in the image of a terrible beast carried this girl, the daughter of a great chief, deep into the forest. She was found lying unconscious on the grass and her dress was torn, baring her body. There is no doubt that her virginity that was sought after by so many most noble young men was violated by the terrible beast. Neither from ancient scrolls, nor from tales of elders, do we know a single case where the devil

---

56   Chlamys is a cloak worn by men in ancient Greece

possessed a Carthaginian maiden. This first one must die. Her body must be thrown into fire and memory of her must be expunged, otherwise her breath will offend terribly the dignity of the goddess Ishtar." He finished, and the other priests bowed their heads in approval. The commanders cast down their eyes, unhappy, but not knowing how to object, and the people howled in frenzied joy. It is always pleasant to take a look at a beautiful maiden's body surrounded by red snakes of flame. However, Gannon did not think that.

By the expression of her eyes and by the corners of the bound girl's mouth, he saw that the priest was wrong and that the forest devil had not had time to carry out his intention. His experienced eyes of a refined man of pleasure could not be mistaken. But it was dangerous to openly contradict the priests; he had to resort to cunning. For a moment he hesitated, but then his eyes glistened, an enigmatic smile covered his lips and, bending forward slightly, he folded his hands on his chest as if he were anticipating some kind of pleasure. "Great priests who know the most treasured mysteries and you, valiant warrior commanders who brought fame to the name of Carthage in distant lands, I am surprised at the measure of your grief. Why do you think that the goddess is offended? Did not she reveal her strength and power in all their glory? Did not she come to aid the favorite of her daughters? The forest devil was found dead, but there was not a single wound on his body! Who besides the Goddess Ishtar strikes bloodlessly with a single breath from her lips? Our wise ancestors taught us that the gods leave their heavenly dwellings and interfere in earthly affairs only for the worthiest of mortals." He thought for a bit and suddenly added unexpectedly, with a gracious smile and a beautiful motion of his hand, "And I, Gannon, the ruler of all lands from Carthage to the Great Waters, I take this girl marked by the grace of the Goddess to be my wife." And he did not regret his words when he saw what a tender subtle blush suddenly covered the cheeks of his chosen one, and what a happy and bashful fire lit up in her eyes, which had been haughty before, and now were bewildered and grateful. The people again howled with joy, but this time more enthusiastically and loudly, because, although the beautiful spectacle had slipped away from them, they knew that the wedding festivities would be accompanied by royal favors and magnificent presents. The sullen priests did not dare to object. While Gannon was afraid of their influence, then they really felt a panicked terror before him.

IV

The dark, terrifying African night quickly enveloped the earth, and the wild odors of wandering beasts were replaced by the scent of flowers and grass. The roar of gold-maned hungry lions could be heard, resembling the crashing sound of falling cliffs. The poisoned arrows of Nubian hunters kept the animals outside the camp. The sudden shrill groan of a doe attacked during its sleep would resound, and it would be echoed by the laughter of hyenas. A large yellow moon was seen over the forest. It was gliding silently and seemed to be a predator of the sky, devouring the stars. The wedding feast was over, torches made out of aloe branches were extinguished, and drunken Negroes were lying around ponderously in the bushes, evoking the contempt of the temperate Carthaginians.

In a white silk tent, Gannon waited for his betrothed, whose body was being anointed with arousing Indian perfumes by skillful slave girls. He was describing the path he traveled so far with a golden stylus on wax boards and marked the quantity of ivory either bought or captured from the natives. To dream and to worry in anticipation of his first conjugal night was not in his character. Having dismissed her slaves, the youthful bride slowly headed for the tent of intimacy. Nervous and blushing, she silently repeated the words that she had to say to her bridegroom upon entering his tent, "Here is your slave, master, do with her as you wish." And the thought about what would come after that clouded her eyes with a pink mist and made her heart beat quickly like a captive bird. Suddenly a strange object loomed black before her. When she approached, she understood what it was. The angered Carthaginians had chopped off the baboon's head and had stuck it on a stake, exhibiting it in the middle of the camp so that every passerby could strike it or spit at it or somehow express his contempt. The glazed eyes blankly stared into space. The skin was soiled with caked blood, but the teeth were bared as before, frenzied and threatening. The girl was startled and stopped. All the amazing events of this day again rushed through her mind. She did not doubt that the goddess Ishtar had really come to her aid and had defeated her enemy so that her maiden's honor could be preserved, so that the ancient family would not be besmirched, so that Gannon himself, as beautiful as the sun, would take her as his wife. But a strange pity was awakened in her for the one who dared to argue for her sake with the Insuperable One and who died such a terrible death. Over what gloomy chasms does his spirit hover? What blood-chilling visions surround it? It is terrifying to die fighting gods, to die without reaching your goal, and to carry the frenzied madness of desire into the darkness forever.

In an impetuous movement, the girl lowered her pale lips to the beast's maw, and the instantaneous chill of the kiss sharply pierced her entire body. Fiery circles swirled before her eyes, her ears became filled with sound that was like the falling of many waters, and when she had recoiled at last she had become totally different.

Unhurriedly, she continued on her path, peaceful and pensive in a new way. Her cheeks no longer flamed and her heart did not shudder when she thought about Gannon. The first virginal impulse of her soul had fallen on the lot of the forest devil who had died because of her.

THE AFRICAN HUNT

I

On ancient vignettes, Africa was often depicted as a young woman who was beautiful despite the coarse simplicity of her forms, and she was always, always surrounded by wild beasts: with monkeys swinging over her head, elephants waving their trunks behind her back, a lion licking her feet, and a panther luxuriating next to her on a cliff warmed by the sun.

Artists failed to cope with the growth of colonization, the building of railroads, with the earthworks for irrigation and drainage—and they were right not to do so. It is here in Europe that it seems to us that the human struggle with nature has ended, or, in any case, the advantage is already, obviously, on our side. For those who have traveled to Africa the matter seems quite different.

Narrow embankments of railroads are washed out every summer by tropical downpours, elephants like to scratch their sides against the smooth surface of telegraph poles, and, of course, break them, and hippos overturn steamships on the river. The Englishmen have been preoccupied for so many years with the conquest of the Somali Peninsula and yet haven't managed to advance even a hundred kilometers from the shore. At the same time, you can't say that Africa is inhospitable. Its forests are equally open for whites as for blacks. As if by silent agreement, man comes to the waterholes before the animals, but Africa expects only guests and never recognizes them as its masters.

A European, if he is lucky to slip through the line of whining skeptics (largely the small tradesmen) in the coastal cities, if he doesn't listen to the sinister warnings of his consul, if he finally manages to gather a caravan that won't be too large and unwieldy, he may see Africa as it was thousands of years ago: unnamed rivers with heavy, leaden waves, deserts where it seems only God dares to raise His voice, forests, hidden in mountain canyons, which are totally rotten and ready to fall from a single push; he will hear how a lion, readying itself for battle, whips its flanks with its tail, and how a claw, hidden in its tail, reverberates when it hits his ribs; he will be amazed by the ancient tribe of the Shangalis, among which a woman does not dare to walk but on all fours in the presence of a man; and if he is a hunter, then he will find game worthy of fabulous princes. But he must equally temper both his body and soul: the body—in order not to fear the desert heat and swamp dampness, all types of wounds, and possible periods of starvation; the spirit—in order not to quiver at the sight of his and others' blood and to accept this new world, so unlike ours, as immense, terrible, and wondrously beautiful.

II

The Red Sea is unquestionably a part of Africa, and a shark hunt in the Red Sea can be a perfect introduction to African hunts.

We anchored near Jedda, where we were not allowed to go because of a plague. I know of nothing more beautiful than the bright green shoals of Jedda, skirted with a slightly pink foam. Might it be that it is in their honor that Hajis, Muslims who visit Mecca, wear green turbans?

While coal was being loaded, it was decided to have a shark hunt. A huge hook with ten pounds of rotting meat tied to a strong cable served as a fishing rod, a log was used for the float. But we could not see any sharks, or maybe they were swimming so far in the distance that their pilot fish couldn't see the lure. A shark is extremely nearsighted, and it is always accompanied by two small pretty fish that direct it to its prey and receive their share for their labor, which is why these fish are called pilots.

Finally, a dark shadow about three meters long appeared in the water, and the float, after spinning a few times, bobbed into the water. We jerked the line, but pulled out just an empty hook. The shark had just tugged on the lure but didn't swallow it. Now, apparently saddened by the disappearance of the appetizingly pungent piece of meat, it swam in circles almost on the surface of the water and splashed its tail. Confused pilot fish were dashing here and there. We hurried to cast the hook again. The shark dashed at it without hesitation. The cable immediately tightened, threatening to break, then went slack, and a round, glossy head with small evil eyes appeared above the water. I had seen such eyes only on old, exceptionally fierce wild boars. Ten sailors were straining laboriously to pull the cable. The shark was spinning madly, and we could hear it strike the side of the ship with its tail and swirled it in the water like a ship's propeller. The captain's mate, leaning over the banister, shot it five times in a row with his revolver. The shark shuddered and grew still. Five black holes appeared on its head and whitish lips. After one more pull, the terrifying carcass was right at the side of the ship. Someone touched it on the head, and it snapped its teeth. It was apparent that the shark was quite strong and gathering strength for the decisive battle. Then, having tied a knife to a long stick, the captain's mate plunged it into the shark's chest with a strong and deft strike, and, straining, made the cut to the tail. Water poured out, mixed with blood; the pink spleen about a meter and a half in size, the spongy liver and intestines fell out and rocked on the water like a strangely-shaped jellyfish.

The shark immediately became lighter and could be easily pulled onto the deck. The ship's cook, armed with an ax, started to chop off its head. Someone pulled out its heart, and it was throbbing, moving back and forth in froglike leaps. The scent of blood was in the air.

In the water, right at the side of the ship, the orphaned pilot fish was scurrying to and fro. Its friend had disappeared, apparently hoping to hide the shame of its involuntary betrayal somewhere in distant lagoons. But this one was inconsolable; loyal to the end, it jumped out of the water, as though wishing to take a look at what was being done to its mistress, circling around the floating entrails, to which other sharks avidly hurried, and expressing its inconsolable despair in every possible way.

The shark's jaws were chopped off in order to pull out its teeth, and the rest was thrown into the sea. That evening, the sunset over the green shoals of Jedda was wide and bright yellow with the crimson spot of the sun in the middle. Then it became gently ash-colored and greenish, as though the sea were reflected in the sky. We raised anchor and headed straight toward the Southern Cross.

III

There, where the Abyssinian plateau changes into the lowland and the scorching desert sun heats large round stones, caves, and low bushes, you can often come across a leopard that had become too lazy from the food of a certain village. Graceful, multi-colored, with thousands of tricks and whims, the leopard plays the role of some splendid and hostile house spirit in the life of the settlers. It steals their cattle and sometimes children. Not a single woman, after going to a spring for water, misses an opportunity to say that she saw it resting on a cliff and that it looked at her as if it were going to attack. Young warriors compare themselves to the leopard in their songs and try to imitate its lightness of a leap. From time to time, some ambitious, enterprising villager goes to hunt it with a poisonous spear, and if he escapes without being maimed, which often happens, then he triumphantly drags the silken skin with an intricate design to a neighboring tradesman to exchange it for a bottle of a bad cognac. A new beast settles in place of the old one, and everything starts anew.

Once, in the early evening, I came to a small Somali village somewhere on the edge of the Harar plateau. My servant, a deft Hararite, immediately ran to an elder to tell him what an important master I was, and he came bringing eggs, milk, and a fine one-and-a-half-year-old goat as a present for me. As usual, I started asking him about the hunt. It turned out that a leopard had wandered onto the slope of a neighboring hill half an hour ago. Since this news was told to me by the elder, it was reliable. I drank my milk and set off. My servant was bringing the goat that we had just received as bait.

We finally came upon the slope that looked like our trash dumps with its faded burnt out grass and small prickly thorn bushes. We tied the goat in the middle of the clearing. I hid in the bush about fifteen steps away, and my Hararite lay down behind me with a spear in his hand. He bugged out his eyes, waved his weapon, trying to convince me that it was the eighth leopard that he would kill. He was a coward, and I ordered him to be silent. We didn't have to wait for long; I thought that the desperate bleating of our goat would attract all the leopards in the area. I suddenly noticed a distant bush moving, a stone swaying, and then I saw the approaching colorful beast the size of a hunting dog. It prowled quickly, pressing its stomach to the ground and waving the tip of its tail silently. Its blunt catlike snout was motionless and threatening. The leopard had an appearance so familiar to me from books and pictures that, at the first instant, I had the incongruous thought that it could have run away from some traveling circus. Then my heart immediately started racing, my body straightened out, and as soon as I took aim, I fired.

The leopard leapt up a meter high and fell heavily on its side. Its hind legs jerked, digging into the ground, the forepaws were tucked in as if it were ready to pounce, but the body was still, and the head dangled to the side more and more; the bullet had broken its spine right below the neck. I understood that I didn't have to worry about it attacking, lowered my rifle, and turned to my *askir*[57], but his place was empty, only the spear that he had thrown down was lying there. And far behind, I noticed a figure in a white shirt desperately rushing in the direction of the village.

I approached the leopard; it was already dead, and its eyes had stopped moving, clouded with whitish murk. I wanted to carry it away, but when I touched this soft body, which seemed to lack any bones, I completely convulsed. I suddenly felt fear, which was growing like a malleable chill, which was apparently the reaction after a burst of strong, nervous emotion. I looked around. It was already growing really dark, only one edge of the sky was somewhat yellow from the rising moon; the bushes rustled their thorns; hills arched from every direction. The goat had run off as far as the tightly stretched rope allowed it, and stood there lowering its head, frozen in terror. It seemed to me that all the animals of Africa were laying in anticipation all around me, just waiting for the moment to kill me in a torturous and shameful way.

But then I heard the rapid stamping of feet and short abrupt shouts, and like a murder of crows, a dozen Somalis flew into the clearing, holding their spears across their bodies. Their eyes were flaring up from the quick run, and drops of sweat shone on their necks and foreheads like glass beads. My Hararite guide ran breathless right behind them. It was he who had roused the whole village with the news of my death.

IV

The river Awash, which is sometimes slow and wide, and sometimes narrow and seething like a mountain stream, is surrounded by forests. Not by gloomy and damp forests, which stretch for hundreds of miles, but by oasis forests, like those about which people sing in folk songs: forests that are full of gurgling streams, shafts of sunlight, and whistling birds. Buffaloes graze on spacious clearings there, while boars lay in wait in bogs and in the undergrowth. From the east and west people come there to hunt, and from the north, lions come from the Danakil desert to do the same.

They rarely come across each other because the former like the day and the latter come during the night. During the day, lions sleep on the hilltops from where, as though from a watchtower, they observe the surrounding area. If a man approaches, they silently crawl down to the other side of the

---

57 An askir is an Abyssinian soldier.

hill and then run off. And at night people surround their camps with a circle of bright bonfires. Therefore, mutual attacks are extremely rare.

Once in the afternoon, in one of those forests where I amused myself by shooting marabous, my servant, an experienced Abyssinian, a huge man with a pockmarked face, showed me tracks right by the water. "Anbassa (a lion)," he said, lowering his voice, "it comes here to drink." I doubted it, saying that if the lion drank here last night, who could guarantee that it would come here tomorrow, but my servant picked up a hard, whitish ball as proof that the lion had come here before, and I was convinced. To kill a lion is the cherished dream of any white man who comes to Africa, whether it be a buyer of resin, a missionary, or a poet. Upon informed deliberation on this issue, we decided to set up a tree stand and to lay there and wait all night. This way the lion could come closer, and it would be better to shoot from above.

A convenient spot was found nearby at the edge of a small clearing. We worked until evening and built a rough slanted stand on which two people could manage to sit with their feet dangling. So as not to take any unnecessary shots, we caught a two-foot-long turtle and ate its liver that we cooked over a small fire. The night found us in our hiding spot.

We waited for a long time. At first we heard the wild boars that had stayed out too late rumble and shuffle in the bushes; then some bird cried out in alarm; finally, it became as quiet as if the entire world had become deserted all at once. Then the moon rose, and we saw a porcupine in the middle of the clearing sniffing at something and digging the ground, but then a hyena cried out boomingly in the distance, and the porcupine scampered away into the thicket. My feet had become terribly numb since we had been sitting in the same position for nearly five hours.

Only a traveler can imagine how fatigued you can become and how badly you may want to sleep. After a few times when I almost fell down from my watchtower, angered, I finally decided to climb down. I thought it would be better to postpone the hunt till the next night and catch a good sleep during the day. I laid face down in the bushes with my rifle next to me. My servant remained up in the tree. As always happens to a really tired person, not sleep, but a heavy numbness overcame me. I couldn't move, but I heard all the distant rustling, I sensed the moon going down and growing pale.

Suddenly I came to as though I had been pushed, only later realizing that it was my servant whispering to me from the tree, "Getta, Getta

(Master, Master)," and at the far end of the clearing I saw a lion, black against the background of dark bushes. It was coming out from the thicket, and I noticed its huge head raised high above its chest that was as wide as a shield. In the next instant, I took a shot. My Mauser roared incredibly loudly in the complete silence, and we could hear, like its echo, the crackle of broken thorn branches and the hurried bounds of the beast running away. My servant had already jumped down from the tree and was standing next to me holding his Berdan rifle, ready to fire.

My sleepiness was gone. The frenzy of the hunt flowed all through us. We circled the clearing through the bushes because we didn't dare walk across it and began to examine the place where the lion had stood. We knew that it would have run away after being shot only if wounded badly or not wounded at all. Striking match after match, we crawled around, looking for drops of blood in the grass, but there were none. The forest wonder had luckily saved its red skin, thunder-like voice, and the menacing voluptuousness of its velvet and steady movements.

V

My friend, a rich young Abyssinian with the title of Liege Adenu, invited me to spend some time at his estate. "Oh, it's only a two-day trip from Addis Ababa," he said, trying to persuade me, "only two days along a good road." I agreed and ordered that my mule be fed and saddled up for the next day. But Liege Adenu insisted that we travel by horseback and brought five horses from his herd.

After I had covered at least a hundred fifty versts[58] with him, I finally understood why he insisted on it so much.

In order to dispel my dissatisfaction caused by fatigue, Liege Adenu came up with the idea of a hunt. Not any hunt, but a battue.[59]

A battue in a tropical forest is an utterly new sensation; you stand waiting and you don't know what will show up from behind a round bush, what will flash between a crooked mimosa and a thick platan tree. You don't know which creature armed with hooves, claws, and teeth will run out

---

58   A verst is an older Russian unit of measurement roughly equal to one kilometer (7/10ths of a mile).

59   The Merriam-Webster dictionary defines battue as: "the beating of woods and bushes to flush game." https://www.merriam-webster.com/dictionary/battue

with its head lowered to be added to your conscience with a bullet. Maybe folktales don't fib, maybe a dragon will appear.

We took our position on two sides of a narrow canyon leading to a dead end. The beaters, about thirty fleet-footed Gallas[60], went deep into the dead-end canyon. We clung to the rocks of nearly completely sheer slopes and listened to the retreating voices of the beaters, which could be heard now from above us, now from below, suddenly merging into a single triumphant roar. The beast had been discovered.

It was a large, striped hyena. It was running on the opposite slope, several meters above Liege Adenu. It was being chased by the chief beater with a club in his hand. He was a thin, muscular, and completely naked Negro. At times, the hyena snapped at him, and then its pursuer would fall a few steps behind it. Liege Adenu and I fired simultaneously. The panting Negro stopped, thinking that his job was done, but the hyena, having toppled over, flying within inches of Liege Adenu, snapping its teeth at him in mid-air, then touching the ground with its paws, somehow managed to stand up and trot away in a businesslike manner. Two more shots finished it off.

In a few minutes, we heard another shout announcing that another beast had been found, but this time the beaters had to deal with a leopard, and they were not as agile as before. Two, three mighty leaps, and the leopard was at the mouth of the canyon. From there, it was free to run off in any direction. We didn't even see it.

A shout echoed for the third time, but it was less concerted this time and was mixed with laughter. A pack of baboons poured out from the canyon. We didn't shoot. It was too amusing to watch these half-dog half-people fleeing with a comic awkwardness that is characteristic only of them among all the other animals. But in the back of the pack there were a few old males with gray manes and gnawing yellow fangs. These, unlike the others, were real beasts in the full meaning of the word, and I shot. One of them stopped, barking hoarsely, and then shut its eyes, slowly falling on its side like a man going to sleep. The bullet had struck its heart, and when we approached, the baboon was already dead. The battue was over.

---

60   "[A] powerful Hamitic people of eastern Africa, scattered over the wide region which extends for about 1000 m. from the central parts of Abyssinia to the neighbourhood of the river Sabaki in British East Africa." https://theodora.com/encyclopedia/g/gallas.html

At night, lying on a straw mat, I thought for a long time why I didn't feel any pangs of conscience about killing animals for amusement and why my blood tie to the world only became stronger because of the killings. That night I had a dream that I was beheaded for my participation in some Abyssinian court coup. Bleeding out, I applauded the skill of the executioner and rejoiced at how simple, good, and painless it all had been.

UPSTREAM ALONG THE NILE

(PAGES FROM A DIARY)

May 9

I've gotten tired of Cairo, of the sun, of the natives, of the Europeans, of the decorative giraffes, and of the evil monkeys. Every night I dream of another country, familiar and beautiful, every night I clearly remember what I must do, but I wake up and forget everything. Days and weeks pass by, yet I am still in Cairo.

May 11

Everything will be decided tomorrow. Today, at the French consul's reception, I met a tall Englishman with an arrogant line marking his lips and childishly merry blue eyes. I was told that he was an artist and was going to travel to the source of the Nile. And, at first sight, I understood that he knew a lot. If, in general, a mystery still exists among Aryan nations, then Englishmen possess it more often than others. I invited him for coffee and anxiously waited for his answer. He promised to come.

May 12

"Would you like a cigar Mr. Thierry?"
"Thank you, Mr. Grant."
"They say there are only malaria and mosquitoes at the source of the Nile."
"Yes, but there is also an especially rare breed of sacred crocodiles, emerald ones."
"The Arabs are more interesting than the Negroes."
"One beggar dervish told me that a tribe of wise Ethiopians under the leadership of King Balthazar is still powerful in the tropical forests."

"It reminds me of Ryder Haggard's novels."

"Not at all! Ryder Haggard was satisfied with meeting ferocious slave merchants, shifty dwarfs, and beautiful maidens with white skin, but we are people of 1906, we look for hidden things and find mysteries where Haggard wouldn't find anything except for a withered palm tree or a sick Negro woman."

"But where is the gold, the purple, and the splendor of the black kings?"

"Do you see this gold coin? Does it really please you? And what about these red silk drapes? Or this rug from old Persia, on which people, perhaps, had cast spells over sun spirits, all of this very crudely conceals deep boredom. And it seems to me that our splendid buildings at any moment can suddenly open up in an irrepressible gigantic yawn. I would be upset if I stumbled upon anything like that during my trip."

"What can you stumble upon then?"

"A new knowledge that would show another side of all things. Find it, and you will be astonished how you can consider a cloud to be an atmospheric phenomenon when it is, in fact, a star-winged butterfly from the kingdom of Giotto's primitivism[61]. And a coconut can tell you more than all the books in the world."

"If you permit it, Mr. Thierry, I'd like to go with you."

"Then you have to hurry, Mr. Grant, I'm leaving at dawn tomorrow."

May 24

We've been traveling for almost two weeks and today landed on the shore near a small pyramid unknown to tourists. Not a soul was around and we entered it without a guide. The stairways were winding, ascending and descending, and suddenly ended up at an enticingly frightening black pit. Mr. Thierry lazily shrugged his shoulders and went upstairs. But I tied a rope to the ledge of a cliff and started to descend holding a tar torch that dropped fiery droplets into the darkness. Soon I reached a cracked, wet bottom and, sitting down on a stone, looked around. My torch illuminated only part of the cave, which was very, very old, yet strangely familiar.

Water was dripping somewhere. Remnants of a mummy that had fallen apart were lying around. A large black snake flashed by and disappeared.

---

61   Giotto is an Italian pre-Renaissance painter whose frescos in Asizi bore the strong influence of medieval art.

"It had never seen the sun," I thought in alarm. A pensive toad crawled from behind a rock and seemingly wanted to approach me but was frightened by the light from the torch.

I suddenly felt sad like never before. In order to distract myself, I approached the wall and started to examine the half-erased hieroglyphic inscription. It was written in the old Egyptian language, which was much older than the Louvre's papyrus scrolls. I had seen similar characters only in the British Museum. But, perhaps, the blessing of the pensive toad had cleared up my mind, because I was able to read and to understand them. It was neither a story of old battles, nor a recipe for preparations for a mummy, these were words full of a sweet intoxicating fire that fell on my soul, transforming it and giving it new insights that allowed me to understand everything.

I cried tears of gratitude and felt that the world will now change, one word. . . and a new sun will begin to dance in the golden azure and all mistakes will turn into flowers.

My torch crackled and began to go out. But I had already read enough. I began to climb up and in the last flicker of the fire, and again I saw the black snake that had flashed fleetingly like a vague warning and the cherished sacred letters.

I easily found Mr. Thierry, who was sitting nearby and painting a dead crocodile. At my approach, he raised his childish, unknowing eyes at me. I smiled and uttered the secret word that I had brought from the depth of the pyramid. The sun began to spin, to jump and roll, like a black sphere, into the abyss. And in its place, words ignited, "You haven't read it to the end, you wretch! And what you've said is poison." I fell to the ground in terror and as though in a dream, I heard an apprehensive earthly voice, "What's wrong with you Mr. Grant?"

June 17

I had spent three weeks lying in bed with a case of severe Nile malaria, and only today I am well enough to take to my diary. Mr. Thierry brought me back to Cairo and nursed me as if I were a child, but it seems he knows something, because, when I told him we have to return to the pyramid, he began to speak of the Neo-Platonists and their sun spells, and finally almost openly said, "Beware of pensive toads."

How does he know?

HAS MENELIK DIED?

Has Menelik died? That is the question on which the fate of the large independent country in Africa depends, ancient Eastern Orthodox Abyssinia, a country with a population of fifteen million. If so, then the mighty feudal lords will begin the fight for the emperor's throne; recently subjugated peoples will rise up; and all this will become a pretext for the Europeans to divide Abyssinia among themselves. This division has already been decided, and, by a secret pact, the French will obtain the eastern provinces, the Italians will get the northern and part of the south regions, and the British will have all the rest. They don't know only what to do with the central part where Lake Tana is located. It serves as a source for the Blue Nile, the main source of irrigation for Egypt. If the Italians take over this lake, they can divert its water to their barren Eritrea, and it will become a new Egypt, and the old one, deprived of water, will merge with the Sahara Desert. The British, of course, cannot agree to that and demand Tana for themselves, although in any case, during the division, they'll get more than anyone else.

If Menelik is alive, then everything will be as before. Ministers from the capital of Abyssinia, Addis Ababa, will rule over the feudal lords, strong garrisons will keep the subjugated tribes in obedience; the whites will not dare attack the incredibly brave and extraordinarily resilient people. European schools, which already exist in Abyssinia, will graduate a number of people capable of governing and cognizant of the dangers that threaten their country, and it will remain independent for many centuries, which it fully deserves.

Let's try to examine this question, and in order to do that, return to the events of 1906. By that time, Menelik had long wanted to break the power of the feudal lords. Those haughty Rases[62] (leaders) sitting tight on their thrones in their mountainous or wooded provinces, willingly recognized him as their ruler, but they didn't want to recognize his favorite

---

62   Ras is an Ethiopian word meaning "head" or "leader."

grandson, the Liege Iyasu, the son of his daughter and of the conquered and then baptized chief Uollo, as his heir. To a large extent, they justifiably maintained that if Menelik didn't want to recognize his sons as his heirs, then the throne should be given to a pure-blooded Abyssinian and a descendent of King Solomon, as was the entire royal family. Menelik dared to make a risky move: he preserved the governors' rights for the Rases in their provinces, but entrusted the entire governance of affairs to ministers whom he chose from among the people loyal to him, although most of them were not of noble origin. Immediately after that, the influential chief Ras Makonnen headed for Addis Ababa with his Harar regiments. He was poisoned on the way. A rebellion flared up in Tigre, and it was suppressed only after bloody battles. The rest of the Rases were in a mild state of unrest, and suddenly a rumor spread that Menelik had died.

I was told terrible things in Addis Ababa. The emperor was given poison, but by the extraordinary exertion of will, he rode a horse all day and overcame the effect of the poison. Then he was poisoned a second time, this time with a slow-acting poison, and they tried to undermine his good spirits with sinister omens of his imminent death. For superstitious Abyssinians, a dead cat foretells the death of a person who sees it. Every evening when he entered his bedroom, the emperor found the corpse of a black cat by his bed, and one night the empress Taitu announced that after the sudden death of Menelik, she would become the ruler and sent troops to arrest the ministers. The latter, after they had beaten back their attackers, gathered for a council in the house of the metropolitan Abuna Mateos, arrested Taitu in the morning, and announced that Menelik was still alive, but sick and unable to see anyone.

Since that time, no one except for the officials could say that they had seen the emperor. Even European ambassadors were not admitted to see him. Ras Tasama, the guardian of the Liege Iyasu, who agreed with the ministers' opinion in everything, ruled in the name of the heir who was still a minor. In courts and during official appearances, as before, everything was decided in the name of Menelik. In churches people prayed for his recovery.

Six years passed this way and Liege Iyasu grew up. Several elephant hunts, several campaigns against the tribes that had not been subjugated yet, and the lion cub's eyes lit up with fire for the emperor's throne. Ras Tasama suddenly died from an illness common among Abyssinian dignitaries: from poison, and one night Liege Iyasu, with his retinue, burst into the emperor's palace to prove that Menelik had died and he could now be crowned. But the government wasn't napping: the Minister of Finance, Haile Georghis, the handsomest and most flamboyant man in Addis Ababa, gathered up people and drove Liege Iyasu out of the palace. Uolde Georghis, the Minister of War, rushed straight from his bed, naked, to the telegraph station and cut the wires with his saber so the whites wouldn't know about the strife in the capital. Liege Iyasu was harshly reprimanded, after which he was supposed to go visit his father in Uollo. The European ambassadors were given a definitive confirmation that Menelik was alive.

Several weeks ago, I again read in newspapers that Menelik had died, and the next day I read the refutation of that rumor. This means that something similar to what I have just described happened once more.

So, is Menelik alive or not? In my opinion, he is alive, because the best part of him—that mighty and united Abyssinia—is alive, and it is the same as he has made it. When it is finally announced that he is dead, he will really die with the independence of Abyssinia, which he symbolizes. They talk of his ancestor, King Solomon, that he compelled spirits to build a temple, and, having felt death approaching, ordered his body tied to the throne so that the spirits wouldn't notice he was dead, and he could continue his work. The same was repeated during our time.

A song is sung across Abyssinia, composed not during the golden days of victories or during the reign of the favorite emperor, but in the mystic days of his second, illusory, existence:

"You cannot escape death; there was an emperor Aba-Dania, but the leopard's eyes hurt, he does not come out from his lair!

Aba-Dania's horse would not become cowardly: a cowardly horse is afraid of its shadow, beginning with an elephant's and ending with a giraffe's.

To whom has he bequeathed his shield? He continues to make threatening gestures, but people hold onto him only out of habit."

THE AFRICAN DIARY

CHAPTER ONE

Once in December 1912, I was in one of those quaint corners of Petersburg University cluttered with books where undergraduate and graduate students, and sometimes even professors, drink tea and make small jokes about each other's areas of expertise. I was waiting for a famous Egyptologist[63] for whom I had brought an Abyssinian diptych as a present from my most recent trip. The diptych was of the Virgin Mary with infant on one side and a saint with his foot cut off on the other. Among people of this select assembly, the diptych had a lukewarm reception: a Classicist talked about its lack of artfulness, a Renaissance scholar about the European influence on it, which devalued it; an ethnographer spoke about the superiority of the art of non-Russian Siberian minorities. They were much more interested in the trip itself, asking me questions which are typical on such occasions: Were there many lions there? Are the hyenas very dangerous? What do the travelers do if they're attacked by the Abyssinians? No matter how much I tried to convince them that you have to spend weeks looking for lions, that hyenas are bigger cowards than hares, and that Abyssinians are very much law-abiding people and do not attack anyone," I saw that they believed me very little. It turned out that it is harder to destroy legends than to create them.

At the end of the conversation, Professor Zh.[64] asked me whether I had already given a lecture about my trip in the Academy of Science.

---

63   Professor B. A. Turaev (1868-1920) was an Egyptologist and an historian of Ethiopian religion. In her memoirs Anna Akhmatova wrote: "The triptych was given to Prof. Turaev."
64   By Professor Zh. Gumilev most likely meant the Academician V. V. Radlov (1837-1918), who would be instrumental in arranging Gumilev's trip to Abyssinia.

I immediately imagined this huge white building with inner courtyards, stairways, alleys—the entire fortress protecting official science from the outside world; workers wearing clothing embroidered with golden lace, trying to find out exactly whom I wanted to see; and finally, the grim face of the secretary on duty, who would declare that the Academy was not interested in private research, the Academy had its own researchers, and continued with similar discouraging phrases. Besides, as a man of literature, I was used to viewing the academicians as my age-old enemies. I related some of these considerations to Professor Zh, in milder form, of course. However, not a half hour later, with a letter of recommendation in my hand, I found myself at the spiral staircase in front of the door to the waiting room of one of the masters of academic destinies.

Five months had passed since then. During this time, I often spent time on the inner stairways, in the spacious offices, crowded with collections that hadn't been sorted out yet, in the attics and basements of the museums of this large white building by the Neva River. I met scholars and scientists who looked as if they had just jumped out of the pages of Jules Verne's novels as well as those who could speak with an enthusiastic glimmer in their eyes about lice and crickets, along with those whose dream was to find the skin of the wild red dog that lived in Central Africa, or those, who like Baudelaire, were ready to believe in the truly divine nature of the tiny wooden and ivory idols. Almost everywhere the reception they provided struck me with its warmth and hospitality. The princes of official science turned out to be like real princes, considerate and benevolent.

I have a dream that endures, despite of all the obstacles in realizing it: to cross the Danakil Desert, which stretches between Abyssinia and the Red Sea, to investigate the lower parts of the Awash River, to meet the mysterious tribes scattered there. Nominally, they are subjects of the Abyssinian ruler, but in fact, they are free. Since they belong to the single tribe of Danakil, quite gifted, although very fierce, after finding access to the sea, they can be united, civilized, or at least Arabicized. That would add a new member to the family of peoples. And access to the sea does exist. It is through Regita, a tiny independent sultanate north of Obock. One Russian adventurer (there are as many of them in Russia as anywhere else) almost acquired it for the Russian government, but our Ministry of Foreign Affairs rejected his proposal.[65]

---

65   This was Colonel L. K. Artamonov (1859-1932), who would later become

My proposed route was not accepted by the Academy. It cost too much. I reconciled myself with this rejection and offered a different route, which was accepted by the Museum of Anthropology and Ethnography of the Imperial Academy of Science after some discussion.

I was to go to Port Djibouti in the Bab al-Mandab Straight, from there by railroad to Harar, then to put a caravan together, to travel south to the area lying between the Somalian Peninsula and Lakes Rudolf, Margaret, and Zwai, to traverse the widest possible area in my investigation, to take photographs, to collect ethnographic items, and to record songs and legends. Besides, I was even given permission to gather zoological collections. I requested to take an assistant with me and chose my relative N. L. Sverchkov, a young man who loved hunting and natural sciences. He was distinguished by such an agreeable character, that out of a desire to preserve peace, he would endure all kinds of hardship and danger.

Preparations for the trip took a whole month of persistent work. We had to get a tent, rifles, saddles, saddlebags, certifications, letters of recommendation, and so forth.

I was so exhausted that I spent the whole day before departure in bed with a fever. The preparation for the trip is indeed more difficult than the trip itself.

We left Petersburg on April 7 and arrived in Odessa on the morning of the 9th.

[Odessa makes a strange impression on a citizen from the north. It looks like some foreign city Russified by a zealous administrator. There are huge cafes filled with suspiciously elegant traveling salesmen. In the evening people walk along Diribasovskaya Street, which at that time resembled Boulevard Saint-Michel in Paris. There is also a unique Odessa dialect, with different stresses on syllables, with the wrong use of cases, with some new and unpleasant expressions. It seems that this dialect best of all expresses the mentality of Odessa, its childishly naive faith in the omnipotence of resourcefulness, its ecstatic desire for success. In a printing shop where I

---

a General in the Russian Imperial Army. In 1897 he reached Obock on a sailboat from Djibouti and entered negotiations with the Sultan of Regatta about a possible transition of his country under Russian governance. When the French Ambassador to Russia sent a note of complaint about Artamonov's actions to the Minister of Foreign Affairs M. N. Muravyov, Artamonov was close to being recalled from Obock as a result of this. He later described his travels in that region in his book *Through Ethiopia to the Shores of the White Nile*.

was printing my business cards, a fresh issue of the local evening newspaper, which was also printed there, caught my eye. When I opened it, I saw a poem by Sergei Gorodetsky, which was printed without his name, with only one line changed. The printing shop manager told me that the poem was brought in by one of the young local poets and was passed off as his own work.

Undoubtedly, Odessa has many perfectly decent people, even by the Russian standard of the word, but it is not they who set the general tone. Tiny, nimbly-moving worms appeared on the decaying corpse of the East, and the future belongs to them. Their names are Port Said, Smirna, and Odessa.][66]

On the 10th of April, we sailed off to sea on the steamship *Tambov* of the Volunteer Fleet.[67] The Black Sea, which was stormy and dangerous only two weeks ago, was now calm as a lake. Waves softly gave way under the thrust of the ship, where an invisible screw was digging, pulsating like the heart of a workingman. You couldn't see the foam, only the pale-green, malachite streak of rippling wake of the water stretching out into the distance. In tightly knit flocks, dolphins were rushing after the ship, sometimes overtaking and then falling behind, and at other times, as if in an uncontrollable fit of gaiety, jumped up, showing their glittering, wet backs. Night fell. The first night on the sea is sacred. Stars that I had not seen for a long time were ablaze. Water gurgled more audibly. Can it be that there are people who have never seen the sea?

The morning of the 12th—Constantinople. It was again the beauty of the Bosphorus, openly decorative, but of which you could never get enough—lagoons, boats with wide Latin sails on which merry Turks were grinning, houses clinging to the slopes of the shores, merlons and towers of ancient fortresses surrounded by cypresses and blooming lilacs, and the sun, the unique Constantinople sun, bright and scorching.

We sailed past a squadron of European nations, brought into the Bosporus Straight to react to disturbances.[68] Immobile and gray, it dully

---

66   These two paragraphs were crossed out by Gumilev in the manuscript.
67   The Volunteer Fleet was created in 1878 to promote trade relations with Western Europe and the USA, but it also established an "oriental" trade route of Odessa to Vladivostok and to Japan and China.
68 A reference to the First Balkans War between Turkey and the coalition of Bulgaria, Greece, Serbia, and Montenegro, which ended very unsuccessfully for Turkey.

threatened the noisy and colorful city. It was eight o'clock, time to play national anthems. We listened as the British anthem resounded, calmly and proudly, the Russian was pious, and the Spanish one sounded so festive and bright as though that entire nation consisted of twenty-year-old men and women who had gathered to dance.

As soon as we had anchored, we got into a Turkish boat and set off for the shore without neglecting the usual pleasure of the Bosphorus to get caught in a wave left by a passing ship and to rock madly in the wake for a few seconds. The usual animation reigned in Galata, the Greek part of the city, where we had moored.[69] But as soon as we crossed the wide wooden bridge, thrown across the Golden Horn, and found ourselves in Istanbul, we were struck by the unusual quietness and desolation. Many shops were locked, cafes empty, and in the streets we almost exclusively came across the elderly and children. The men were at Chetaldje. The news of the defeat of Scutteri had just been received.[70] Turkey accepted it with the same calmness with which a hunted and wounded animal accepts a new blow.

We went to Hagia-Sofia along narrow and dusty streets, past silent houses, in every one of which you suspect there were fountains, roses, and beautiful women like in *One Thousand and One Nights*. Half-naked children played in the shady courtyard surrounding the cathedral. Several dervishes were sitting by the wall, deep in meditation.

Contrary to the norm, there was not a single European to be seen.

We folded back the mat hanging in the doorway and entered the cool, semi-dark hallway encircling the temple. A gloomy doorman put leather shoes on our feet so that our feet would not defile the sacredness of this place. One more door, and the heart of Byzantium was in front of

---

69   Galata was a suburb of Istanbul (which Gumilev exclusively calls Constantinople) populated mostly by Greeks, who were all sympathizers of the Balkan coalition. It was separated from Turkish Istanbul by the Golden Horn strait and connected with it by two bridges – an old wooden one and a new draw bridge.

70   Gumilev arrived in Turkey toward the end of the first Balkan war (October 1912 – May 1913), in which the Balkan Alliance, consisting of Bulgaria, Greece, Serbia, and Montenegro, was pitted against the Ottoman Empire. After initial successes of the Allies, the Turks were able to stop their advance at the Chetalji Heights, a few dozens kilometers to the West of Istanbul. After a short ceasefire period, the Allies resumed their advance and captured Janina and Adrianople, and in Albania the Montenegrins and Serbs reached the Adriatic Sea and stormed and captured the city of Scutari after a short siege.

us. There were neither columns, nor stairways, nor alcoves, nor the easily accessible beauty of the Gothic Cathedrals, only space and its well-ordered proportions. It seemed the architect had as his goal to sculpture the air. Forty windows under the dome seemed silver from the light penetrating through them. Narrow piers were supporting the dome, creating the impression that it was unbelievably lightweight. Soft carpets muffled the sound of our footsteps. On the walls, we could see the shadows of angels that the Turks had tried to paint over. A small gray-haired Turk in a green turban hung around us persistently for a long time. Perhaps he kept watch to make sure our shoes wouldn't come off. He showed us a notch in the wall, made by the sword of Sultan Mohammed; the trace of his hand was stained in blood on the wall, the wall into which, according to legend, the Patriarch entered with the Holy Ghost when the Turks had come. We felt bored with his explanations and went out. We paid for the shoes, paid the uninvited guide, and I insisted on going back to the ship.

I'm not a tourist. After visiting Hagia-Sofia, why would I need the buzzing bazaar with its silken and beaded temptations, coquettish parries, or even the incomparable cypresses of the Sulemania Cemetery?[71] I was going to Africa, and I had said the Lord's Prayer in the most sacred of all cathedrals. Several years ago, I was also on my way to Abyssinia. I threw a *louis d'or*[72] into the crevasse of a temple of the palladium of Athena at the Acropolis and believed that the goddess would invisibly accompany me. Now I had become older and wiser.

In Constantinople one more passenger joined us. It was a Turkish consul who had been appointed to Harar. He and I had long conversations about Turkish literature and Abyssinian customs, but more often about foreign policy. He was a very inexperienced diplomat and a great dreamer. He and I agreed to suggest that the Turkish government send instructors to the Somali Peninsula to organize an irregular army from among the Muslims who lived there. It could serve to subdue the Arabs of Yemen, who were constantly revolting, especially since the Turks couldn't handle the Arabian heat.

After two or three more projects of the same sort, we were in Port Said. Disappointing news awaited us there. It turned out that there was cholera

---

71   The ancient cemetery in the old part of Istanbul near the famous Suleiman Mosque.

72   Louis d'or is a series of French coins introduced by Louis XIII in 1640.

in Constantinople, and we were prohibited from having contact with the people of the city. Arabs brought us provisions, which they passed along to us without coming aboard, and we entered the Suez Canal.

Not everyone can love the Suez Canal, but those who fall in love with it, fall in love for a long time. This narrow strip of still water has a completely special, melancholy beauty.

On the African shore, where the houses of the Europeans are scattered about, there are thickets of crooked mimosas with suspiciously dark vegetation, as though it had grown after a fire, and undersized, thick banana palms; on the Asian shore—waves of ashen-red, scorching sand. A chain of camels would pass by slowly, jingling their bells. Some kind of animal would show up from time to time, a dog, or perhaps a hyena or a jackal. It would look at us with hesitation and then run away. Large white birds would fly in circles above the water and sit on the rocks. Here and there, semi-clad Arabs, dervishes, or just the poor who couldn't find a place for themselves in the city, would sit near the water and look at it without taking their eyes off as if they were casting a spell. Other steamships moved in front of and behind us. At night, when projector lamps were turned on, it looked like a funeral procession. We often had to stop in order to let another ship pass by that was moving, slowly and silently like a preoccupied pedestrian, in the opposite direction. These quiet hours on the Suez Canal calmed and lulled the soul into being taken unawares later by the tempestuous and wild beauty of the Red Sea.

The hottest of all the seas, it presents a formidable and beautiful sight. Its water, like a mirror, reflects the nearly sheer rays of the sun, as though there is molten silver above and below it. You are dazzled, and your head spins. Mirages often happen here, and near the shore I saw several wrecked ships that had been deceived by them. Islands, steep barren cliffs, are scattered here and there, looking like unknown African beasts: especially one of them that looks like a lion readying for a leap; it seems you can see its mane and drawn-out snout. These islands are uninhabited because of the lack of drinking water. If you go to the side of the ship, you can see the water, pale blue like the eyes of a murderer. From time to time, strange flying fish leap out of the water, frightening us with the unexpectedness of their jumps. The night is even more beautiful and sinister. The constellation of the Southern Cross hangs somewhat crooked in the sky, which is covered with a golden rash of countless stars, as if stricken with a marvelous sickness. In the west, streaks of sheet lightning flash: it is the tropical storms that burn forests and destroy entire villages deep into Africa. In the foam that the ship leaves behind, whitish sparks gleam: this is the glimmer of the sea. The afternoon heat had abated, but an unpleasant, damp stuffiness was left in the air. You could go onto the deck and be lost in an uneasy slumber full of fantastic and whimsical nightmares.

We anchored in front of Jedda, where we were not allowed to go because of the plague. I know of nothing more beautiful than the bright green shoals of Jedda, skirted with a slightly pink foam. Might it be that it is in their honor that Hajis, Muslims who visit Mecca, wear green turbans?[73]

While the company's agent prepared various papers, the captain's first mate decided to take us shark hunting. A huge hook with ten pounds of rotting meat tied to a strong cable served as a fishing rod, a log was used for a float. We spent more than three hours in tense anticipation.

At times we could not see any sharks, at other times the sharks were swimming so far in the distance that their pilot fish couldn't see the lure.

A shark is extremely nearsighted. Therefore, it's always accompanied by two small pretty fish who direct it to its prey. Finally, a dark shadow about three meters long appeared in the water, and then the float, after spinning a couple of times, dove under the surface. We jerked the rope, but pulled out just the empty hook. The shark only pulled at the lure and didn't swallow it. Now, apparently saddened by the disappearance of the appetizingly pungent piece of meat, it swam in circles almost on the surface of the water and splashed its tail. Confused pilot fish were dashing here and there. We hurried to cast the hook again. The shark dashed at it without hesitation. The cable immediately tightened, threatening to break, then it went slack, and a round glossy head with small evil eyes appeared above the water. Ten shipmates were laboriously pulling the cable. The shark was spinning madly, and we could hear it strike the side of the ship with its tail. The captain's mate, leaning over the side of the ship, shot it five times in a row with his revolver. The shark shuddered and grew still. Five black holes appeared on its head and whitish lips. With a little more effort, it was pulled right up to the side of the ship. Someone touched it on the head, and it snapped its teeth. It was apparent that the shark was quite strong and preparing itself

---

[73] The main event in the life of Moslems is their pilgrimage (hadj) to Mecca. Those who have accomplished it wear the green turban. Unlike Gumilev's poetic version of the symbolism of the green color, it symbolizes not the geographical location, but rather the "green banner of the Prophet."

for the decisive battle. Then, having tied a knife to a long stick, the captain's mate plunged it into the shark's chest with a strong and deft strike, and straining, made the cut to the tail. Water poured out, mixed with blood; the pink spleen about a meter and a half in size, the spongy liver, and intestines fell out and rocked on the water like a strangely-shaped jellyfish. The shark immediately became lighter and could be easily pulled onto the deck. The ship's cook, armed with an ax, started to chop its head. Someone pulled out its heart and threw it on the floor. It was pulsating, moving here and there in froglike leaps. The smell of blood was in the air.

In the water, right at the side of the ship, the orphaned pilot fish was rushing to and fro. Its friend had disappeared, apparently hoping to hide the shame of its involuntary betrayal somewhere in distant lagoons. But this one, loyal to the end, jumped out of the water, as though wishing to take a look at what was being done to its mistress, and circled around the floating entrails, which were already being approached by other sharks with quite obvious intentions, and expressed its inconsolable despair in every possible way.

The shark's jaws were chopped off in order to tear out the teeth, and the rest was thrown into the sea. The sunset over the green shoals of Jedda that evening was wide and bright yellow with the crimson spot of the sun in the middle. Then it became gently ash-colored and greenish, as though the sea were reflected in the sky. We raised the anchor and headed straight toward the Southern Cross. In the evening, I was given three white jagged teeth of the shark, which were my share. In four days, after we passed the unfriendly Bab al-Mandab, we stopped at Djibouti.

CHAPTER TWO

Djibouti lies on the African shore of the Aden Bay, to the south of Obock, on the edge of the Gulf of Tadjoura. On most geographical maps, only Obock is marked, but it has now lost all significance. Only one stubborn European lives there, and sailors, not without reason, say that Obock has been swallowed by Djibouti. The future belongs to Djibouti. Its trade continues to grow, as does the number of Europeans who live there. About four years ago, when I went there for the first time, there were three hundred of them. Now, there are four hundred. But it will completely mature only when the railroad connecting it to the capital of Abyssinia, Addis Ababa, is completed. Then it will win over even Massawa because in the south of Abyssinia there are many more usual items for export than in other parts of this country: ox skins, coffee, gold, and ivory. It's a pity that the French own the railroad, because they are very careless with their colonies and think that they have fulfilled their duty if they send a few officials there who are totally alien to the country and don't like it. The railroad isn't even subsidized.

We went from the ship to the shore in a motorboat. It's an innovation. Earlier, this purpose was served by skiffs paddled by naked Somalis, who used to argue, make jokes, and from time to time, jump into the water like frogs. On the flat shore, white houses were scattered here and there. The governor's palace towered on a cliff in the middle of a garden of coconut and banana palms. We left our luggage at customs and went to the hotel on foot. There we found out that the train, which we were supposed to take to the interior of the country, departed only on Tuesdays and Saturdays. That meant we had to spend three days in Djibouti.

I wasn't very upset about this delay because I love this town and its peaceful and uncomplicated life. From twelve to four in the afternoon the streets seem desolate; all the doors are shut, and only an occasional Somali from time to time drags himself along like a drowsy fly. During these hours, one is supposed to sleep as he would do at night in our country. But then from God knows where carriages appear, even cars, driven by Arabs in colorful turbans, the white helmets of the Europeans, and even the bright dresses of women going to visit someone. The porches of both cafes are filled with people. A dwarf[74] walks among the tables. He is a twenty-year-old Arab under a meter tall, with a child's face and a huge squished head. He doesn't ask for anything but if given a piece of sugar or small change, he thanks you seriously and politely, with a very special Oriental grace that has been developed over centuries. Then everybody goes for a walk. The streets are enveloped in soft early evening twilight, in which houses are outlined very distinctly, built in the Arab style with flat roofs and merlons, with round embrasures and doors in the shape of a key-hole, with terraces, arcades, and other embellishments—everything is covered with a blindingly bright whitewash. During one such evening, we undertook a delightful trip

---

74 We use the word commonly used in Gumilev's time here in English instead of the currently preferred usage of "little person."

to a country garden, in the company of Mssr. Galeb, a Greek businessman, the Russian vice-consul, the latter's wife, and Mozarbei, the Turkish consul, about whom I spoke earlier. In the garden, there were narrow paths among the platan trees and wide-leafed banana palm trees, the buzzing of large beetles, and the warm air, like in a greenhouse, filled with various aromas. One could barely see water glistening at the bottom of deep stone wells. Here and there one could see a mule or a short, hunch-backed zebu tied to a fence. As we were leaving, an old Arab brought a bouquet of flowers and pomegranates, which, alas, weren't yet ripe.

The three days in Djibouti passed quickly. Strolls in the evening, lying about on the beach during the day with futile attempts to catch a crab—crabs run surprisingly quickly, sideways, and at the slightest alarm hide in the briars—and work in the morning. In the morning Somalis of the Issa tribe would come to my hotel, and I recorded their songs. From them I also found out that this tribe had its own king *ogas* Hussein, who lived in the village of Haraua, three hundred kilometers to the southwest from Djibouti; that the tribe was at constant war with Danakils, who lived to the north of them and, alas, was always defeated by the latter; that Djibouti (Hamadu in Somali) was built in place of an unpopulated oasis; that a few days' travel from it there were still people who worshipped black stones, but the majority was still devout Muslims. Europeans who knew the country well also told me that this tribe was considered one of the most ferocious and cunning in all of East Africa. They usually attacked during the night and massacred everyone without exception. One should not trust guides from this tribe.

The Somalis show particular discernment in selecting ornaments for their shields and vessels, in the workmanship of necklaces and bracelets. They are even considered trendsetters in fashion among the surrounding tribes, but they don't have any poetic aptitude. Their songs are awkward in conception, poor in imagery, and are nothing in comparison with the majestic simplicity of Abyssinian songs or the delicate lyricism of Gallasian songs. I will give one love song as an example, the text of which in Russian transcription is given in the appendix.

THE SONG

"Berringa, where the Issa tribe lives, Gurti, where the Gurgura tribe lives, Harar, which is higher than the land of the Danakils, the Galbet people, who don't ever leave their homeland, short people, the country where Isaac reigns, the country on the other side of the river Sellel, where Samarron reigns, the country, where the Gallas carry water from wells on the other side of the river Webi[75] for the chief Darot—I have traveled the whole world, but Marian Magana is more beautiful than all of this, be blessed, Reraudal, where you are more modest, more beautiful, and more pleasant with the color of your skin than all Arab women."

It is true, that all primitive peoples love to include lists of familiar names in their poetry, let's recall, for example, Homer's list of ships, but Somalian lists are cold and lack diversity.

Three days passed. On the fourth day, while it was still dark, an Arab servant, carrying a candle, walked through the hotel rooms, waking up those who were going to Dire Dawa. Still sleepy, but pleased with the morning coolness, which was so pleasant following the afternoon's blinding heat, we set out for the railroad station. Our luggage was brought there beforehand in a hand truck. A trip by second-class ticket costs 62 francs per person, which is rather expensive for a few hours of travel, but all colonial railroads are like this. All the Europeans usually travel in this class since third class is designated for the locals and first class is twice as expensive and no better than second. Only members of diplomatic missions and a few German snobs buy tickets in first class. The locomotives have thundering names, but are far from appropriate: Elephant, Buffalo, Strong One, and the like. Just a few kilometers from Djibouti, while the train was going uphill, we were traveling at a speed of one meter per minute, and two Africans walked in front, pouring sand on the rails, which were wet from the rain.

The view from the window was gloomy but quite majestic. The desert was brown and coarse. Weathered mountains were all in crevices and dotted with chasms, and because it was the rainy season, there were muddy streams and entire lakes of dirty water. A small Abyssinian gazelle dig-dig ran out from the bush; a pair of jackals that always travel in pairs looked at us with curiosity. Somalis and Danakils with huge, disheveled hair stood, leaning on their spears. Only a small part of the country has been explored

---

75   Also known as the Webi Shebelle River.

by Europeans, precisely that part served by the railroad. It's a mystery what is to the right and to the left of it. At small stations, naked black children stretched their tiny hands to us, and dolefully drawled out in sing-song the most popular word in the East: *bakshish*, which means a "present."

At two in the afternoon, we arrived at Aisha Station, two-hundred-and-sixty kilometers from Djibouti, that is, halfway to our destination. A Greek innkeeper there prepared a quite decent breakfast for the travelers. The Greek turned out to be a patriot, and received us, the Russians, with outstretched arms, gave us the best seats, served us himself, but alas, out of the same feeling of patriotism, treated our friend, the Turkish consul, extremely inhospitably. I had to take the host aside and appropriately reprimand him, which was very difficult to do because besides Greek he spoke only a little Abyssinian.

After breakfast, we were told that the train could go no further because rains had washed out the railbed, and the rails were hanging in mid-air. Some let loose their anger, but how could that help at all? The rest of the day was spent in wearisome waiting. Only the Greek failed to hide his joy: he could serve not only breakfast, but dinner as well. At night, everybody settled in the way they could. My traveling companion remained asleep in the railroad car, but I carelessly accepted the invitation of the French conductors to sleep in their room, where there was a free bed, and until the middle of the night I had to listen to their absurd, barracks-room chatter. In the morning, we found out that the railway not only had not been repaired, but that at least eight days were needed before we could move on, and that those who so desired could return to Djibouti. Everyone wished to do that, except for the two of us and the Turkish consul. We stayed because living at the Aisha Station cost much less than in the city. The Turkish consul did it, I think, only out of a sense of friendship, besides the three of us had the vague hope of getting to Dire Dawa in less than eight days. In the afternoon, we went for a walk. We climbed over a small hill covered with small sharp stones, which ruined our shoes forever, chased a big prickly lizard, which we finally caught, and, without noticing, moved about three kilometers from the station. The sun was setting, and we had already turned back when we suddenly saw two Abyssinian station guards who were running toward us waving their weapons. *Myndernu* (What's the matter?), I asked after I saw their alarmed faces. They explained that the Somalis in this area were very dangerous. They threw their spears into passers-by from ambush partly as mischief, partly because according to their custom, only a man who had killed another man could marry. However, they never attacked an armed person. Later, the truthfulness of these stories was confirmed to me, and with my own eyes I saw in the village of Dire Dawa children throwing a bracelet up into the air and piercing it with a deftly thrown spear while the ring was still in the air. We returned to the station escorted by the Abyssinians who suspiciously looked over every bush, every pile of stones.

The next day, a train with engineers and laborers arrived from Djibouti to repair the railway. On the same train, a courier arrived, carrying mail for Abyssinia.

By that time, it became known that the railway was damaged over an eighty-kilometer stretch, but you could try to get through on a hand-trolley. After wrangling for a long time with the chief engineer, we obtained two hand-trolleys, one for us, and one for the luggage. We had room for *askirs* (Abyssinian soldiers), intended for our protection, and the courier. Fifteen tall Somalis rhythmically shouting: *Aidehe, aidehe*—in the manner of the Russian *dubinushka* ("little club"), which is not a political song, but rather a laborer's one[76]—took up the handles of the handcars, and we set off.

The road was indeed difficult. The rails shook and bent over the gullies, and in some places, we had to go on foot. The sun was so scorching that our hands and necks were covered with boils in half an hour. From time to time, strong gusts of wind sprayed us with dust. The surroundings were quite rich with game. Again we saw jackals, gazelles, and even several marabous on the shore of one of the marshes, but they were too far away. One of our *askirs* managed to kill a buzzard, which was almost the size of a little ostrich. He was very proud of his luck.

In a few hours, we encountered a train with two flatbed cars, which was bringing materials for railway repairs. We were invited to ride with them, and for an hour, we traveled in this primitive way. Finally, we met up with a railroad car that was supposed to take us to Dire Dawa the next morning. We dined on pineapple jelly and cookies, which we happened to have, and spent the night at the station. It was cold, and the roar of hyenas could be

---

76   Gumilev refers here to two versions of the popular folk work song "Dubinushka," which literally means "a little wooden club." The original version became known as a song of the Volga *burlaks* (workers who pulled barges upstream along the Volga River. The second version intensified the political aspects of the song, such as turning a club against the exploiting classes.

heard, but at eight in the morning, we could catch sight of the white houses of Dire Dawa in a grove of mimosas.

What does a traveler who diligently enters his impressions in a diary have to do? How can he acknowledge the first thing that attracts his attention when he enters a new city? Could it be clean beds with white sheets, breakfast at a table, covered with a tablecloth, books, and the opportunity for a pleasant rest?

I'd never deny the celebrated beauty of the "knolls and streams." The sunset in the desert, crossings of the flooded rivers, dreams during the night spent beneath a palm tree: all of these will forever remain the most exciting and beautiful moments of my life. However, when the cultured everyday life, which had managed to become a fairy tale for the traveler, instantaneously turns into reality—let the urban lovers of nature laugh at me—I say it is also beautiful. That's why now with gratitude I remember that gecko, the tiny, completely transparent lizard that was running along the walls of the rooms, and, while we were eating breakfast, was catching mosquitoes above our heads, from time to time turning its ugly but incredibly funny face toward us.

It was time for us to put a caravan together. I decided to take servants from Dire Dawa and to buy mules in Harar where they were much cheaper. The servants were found very quickly: Haile, an African from the Mongali tribe, who spoke French terribly but animatedly, was hired as a translator. Abdulaie, a Hararite who knew only a few French words, but had his own mule to make up for that, was hired as chief of the caravan, and a couple of fleet-footed African vagrants were taken on as *askirs*. Then we hired riding mules for the next day and could go for a stroll through the city with a clear conscience.

Dire Dawa had grown considerably during the three years that I had not seen it, especially its European part. I remember the time when there were only three streets, now there are almost a dozen. There were gardens with flowerbeds, spacious cafes; there was even a French consul. The entire city was divided into two parts by the bed of the dried-out river that filled up only when it rained: the European part, which was located closer to the railroad station, and the native side, that is, a disorderly heap of little huts, pens for cattle, and a few shops. The French and Greeks lived in the European part. The French were the masters of the situation: they were either working at the railroad, where they received good wages, or ran the best hotels, conducting the largest trade; the postmaster was French, the doctor was French as well. They were very respected, but not loved because of their constant arrogance toward the colored races. The Greeks and sometimes the Armenians controlled all of Abyssinia's retail trade. The Abyssinians called them "Grik," and singled them out from the other Europeans, whom they called "Frendjies." They were not accepted, with a few exceptions, in the European, that is, French society, although many of them were quite prosperous. In one small Greek cafe, which in the evening turned into a real gambling house, I saw bets of several hundred thalers made by rather suspicious ragamuffins.

There were neither carriages nor street lamps in the European part of the city. The streets were illuminated by the moon and the windows of the cafes.

You could spend the day wandering through the native part of the city without getting bored. In two large shops, which belonged to two rich Hindus, called Giovaji and Mohammed-Ali, you could see silk, embroidered gold clothes, crescent-shaped sabers in red leather scabbards, daggers with silver embossing, and all kinds of Oriental jewelry, so pleasing to the eye. They were sold by self-important, corpulent Hindus in blindingly white shirts and robes and flat silk hats. The Yemen Arabs ran by, they were also tradesmen, but mostly commission agents. Somalis, skillful in all kinds of craft, wove straw mats and made sandals to measure, right at the same spot. When you walked in front of the huts of the Gallas, you could smell incense, their favorite method of fumigation. In front of the house of Danakil Magadras (properly speaking, the head of the merchants, but in reality, simply an important chief), elephants' tails were hanging, of beasts that were killed by his *askirs*. In the old days tusks used to hang there as well, but since the time when the Abyssinians had conquered the country, the poor Danakils now had to be content with just the tails. The Abyssinians with rifles over their shoulders amble idly with an air of arrogance. They are conquerors, therefore to work is beneath their dignity. Right outside the city, the mountains begin, where families of baboons gnaw at the bushes of milkweed and birds with huge red beaks fly.

In order to be sure of one's *askirs*, you need to register them and their guarantors at the town judge's office. I went to see him and had the opportunity to witness an Abyssinian trial. On the porch of the house, overlooking a fairly spacious courtyard, a stately Abyssinian was sitting with his legs under him. He was the chief judge, surrounded by his assistants and just friends. About five steps in front of him, a log was lying on the ground, over which the litigants could not step over, even in the heat of defense or prosecution arguments. The courtyard was filled with *askirs* in the employ of the judge, as well as with simply curious people. When I entered, the judge politely greeted me, ordered that a chair be brought for me, and when he noticed that I was interested in the trial, provided me with some explanations. On the other side of the log there were standing a tall Abyssinian with a beautiful face, which was distorted with anger, and a stocky Arab, who was filled with the triumph of the expected near victory with one of his feet on a log. The court case consisted of the fact that the Abyssinian had taken the Arab's mule to go somewhere, and it had died. The Arab demanded payment for the mule, and the Abyssinian argued that the mule had been sick. They took turns to speak. The Abyssinian jumped several times over the log and poked his finger nearly into the judge's face. The Arab was assuming commanding poses, was opening and closing his *shama* (a white robe that is common dress for all inhabitants of Abyssinia), and when he was speaking, he chose his phrases well and apparently was performing for the spectators. As a result, in fact, concerted, commiserating laughter accompanied his speeches. Even the judge muttered with a smile: "Oyu goot" (This is amazing). Finally, when both litigants swore on Menelik's death (in Abyssinia, people always swear by the death of the emperor or some high dignitary), insisting on two opposite things, everybody was extremely delighted. I didn't wait until the end, and I left after I had registered my *askirs*, but it was evident that the Arab would win. It is quite difficult to take legal action in Abyssinia. Usually the person who gives a better present to the judge beforehand wins. But how do you find out how much your opponent has given? It doesn't pay to give too much either. Nevertheless, the Abyssinians really love to litigate, almost every argument ends with a traditional oath to a summons in the name of Menelik (*ba Menelik*) to appear in court.

In the afternoon, there was a downpour so severe that the roof was blown off of one of the Greek hotels, which, to say the truth, wasn't a very sturdy structure. Toward the evening, we went for a walk and of course to take a look at what had happened to the river. It was unrecognizable—it was seething like a stream at a mill. One of the branches of the river, which curved around a little island in front of us, was particularly turbulent. Huge waves of absolutely black water, not even water, but of dirt and sand raised up from the bottom, were flying, rolling one over another and smashing against the bend of the shore, going backward, rising straight up in a pillar, and roaring. During that quiet, inundated evening it was a terrifying but beautiful spectacle. A large tree stood right in front of us on the island. At every strike, the waves revealed its roots, spraying it with the splotches of foam. The tree shuddered with all its branches but stood fast. There was almost no ground left under it, only two or three roots held it in place. The spectators even placed their bets on whether the tree would remain standing or not. But then another tree that the stream had washed out somewhere in the mountains was swept into it, butting it like a ram. A dam formed immediately, which was enough for the waves with all their weight to come down on the dying tree. Amid the roar of the water, you could hear the main root snap, the tree slightly swayed and all at once plunged into the whirlpool with its entire green broom of branches. The waves madly picked it up and in a moment it was already far in the distance. During the same time, while we were watching the death of the tree, downstream from us, a child had drowned, and the entire evening we could hear his mother wailing.

In the morning, we set out for Harar.

CHAPTER THREE

For the first twenty kilometers, the road to Harar follows the bed of the same river I mentioned in the previous chapter. Its sides are quite steep, and God forbid the traveler should find himself in it during rain. Fortunately, we were spared that kind of danger because the time interval between the two fortuituous rainfalls lasted about forty hours. We were not the only ones who used this convenient opportunity. Dozens of Abyssinians were traveling the same road, Danakils passed by, Gallasian women with dangling naked breasts were carrying bundles of wood and grass into the city. Long caravans of camels tied together head to tail, as though they were comical beads strung together, frightened our mules as they passed by. In Dire Dawa, they were expecting the arrival of the Dejazmach Tafari, and we often encountered groups of Europeans who had come to meet him, riding on their handsome, frisky horses.

The road resembled the paradise depicted on Russian peasant *lubok* woodcuts: unnaturally green grass, trees with branches that spread too far, large multi-colored birds, and flocks of goats on mountain slopes. The air was soft and transparent, as though pierced with specks of gold. The flowers smelled sweet and strong. Only black people, as if sinners walking in paradise according to some legend that hadn't been created yet, existed in strange disharmony with the entire surroundings.

We were riding at a trot, and our *askirs* were running in front of us, still finding time to fool around and joke with the women who were passing by them. The Abyssinians are famous for their fleetness of foot, and there was a general rule that over a long distance the pedestrian would always overtake a rider. After two hours of travel, the road started to rise: a narrow path that at times almost became a ditch, wound almost perpendicularly up the mountain. Large stones had fallen and blocked the road, and we had to dismount our mules and walk on foot. It was difficult but felt good. We had to run up almost without stopping, keeping our balance on sharp stones, because you don't tire as quickly this way. My heart was beating rapidly, and it was taking my breath away, as if I were rushing to a date. And then you'd be rewarded by the fresh scent of a mountain flower, unexpected as a kiss, by an open view to a softly misted valley that suddenly opened up. When finally, out of breath and exhausted, we ascended the last ridge, water, which we hadn't seen calm for such a long time, flashed in our eyes like a silver shield—it was the mountain lake Adeli. I looked at my watch: the ascent had lasted an hour and a half. We were at the Harar plateau. The surroundings changed dramatically. There were banana palms and molachi hedges instead of mimosas, diligently cultivated fields of durro instead of wild grass. In the Galassa village, we bought *injera* (a type of thick pancake made from black dough which is used in Abyssinia instead of bread) and ate them, surrounded by curious children, who at our slightest movement would start running away. There was a straight road going from there to Harar, and at certain places along it there were bridges thrown across the deep crevasses in the earth. We passed the second lake, Oromolo, which was twice the size of the first one. We shot a marsh bird with two white burrs on its head, spared a beautiful ibis, and in five hours found ourselves before Harar.

Even from the mountain, Harar presented a majestic view with its houses made of red sandstone, tall European buildings, and sharp minarets of mosques. The city is surrounded by a wall, and passage through its gate is not allowed after sunset. Inside, it quite like Baghdad at the time of Harun al-Rashid.⁷⁷ Narrow streets that at times descend and at times ascend like steps, heavy wooden doors, squares filled with crowds of people all dressed in white making a terrible din, court trials there on the same square—all of this is very much filled with the charm of old fairy tales. Petty swindling, which happens in the city, also happens in the spirit of ancient times. A boy walked directly toward us with a rifle on his shoulder. He was a Negro, about ten years old. By all signs he was a slave, and an Abyssinian was watching him from behind a corner. He didn't make way for us, but because we were riding at a trot, it was easy for us to ride around him. Presently, a handsome Hararite appeared. He was apparently in a hurry because he was galloping. He shouted to the boy to make way. The boy didn't listen, and when the mule brushed him, he fell on his back like a wooden soldier, maintaining the same calm seriousness on his face. The Abyssinian who was watching the boy rushed after the Hararite and jumped onto his horse behind his saddle like a cat. "Ba Menelik—you've killed a man." The Hararite had already lost heart, but at that time the black boy, who apparently was tired of lying around, got up and started to shake the dust off himself. The Abyssinian, however, managed to extract a thaler for the maiming nearly dealt to his slave.

We stayed at the Greek hotel, the only one in town, where for a bad room and even lousier board, we were asked to pay a price worthy of the Grand Hotel in Paris. Nevertheless, it was pleasant to drink refreshing peppermint⁷⁸ tea and to play a game of chess with soiled, chipped pieces.

I met some acquaintances in Harar. The suspicious Maltese Caravana, the former bank official with whom I had a terrible row in Addis Ababa, was the first to come greet me. He tried to pass off someone else's bad mule on me, hoping to receive a commission. He also suggested playing poker, but I already knew the way he played. Finally, with monkey-like grimaces, he suggested sending a case of champagne to the Dejazmach in order to drop in on him later and boast about his effectiveness. When he failed to engage me in any of his urging, he lost all interest in me. As for me, I sent to look for my other Addis Ababa acquaintance, a small,

---

77   A reference to the character from *1001 Nights*.
78   The original here is "pintserment" in the genitive case. I have been unable to find the word in any dictionaries and have decided to translate it as peppermint tea here since the Vladimir Dal' dictionary lists "piperment" as a Russian spelling for peppermint in the time of Gumilev.

fastidious, middle-aged Copt, who was the principal of a local school. Inclined toward philosophizing, like the majority if his compatriots, he sometimes expressed interesting thoughts, told amusing stories, and his entire world view made the impression of good, stable balance. We played poker, visited his school where little Abyssinians from the best families in town composed arithmetic exercises in French. In Harar, we even found our compatriot, a Russian subject, Artyom Iohandjian, the Armenian who used to live in Paris, America, and Egypt, and now for almost twenty years had been living in Abyssinia. On his business cards, he was listed as a medical doctor, a doctor of science, a merchant commission negotiator, a businessman, and a former member of a court, but when he was asked how he managed to receive so many titles, the answer was a vague smile and complaints about hard times.

Those who think that it's easy to buy mules in Abyssinia are very much mistaken. There aren't any special mule merchants or mule markets. *Askirs* walk from house to house, asking if there are any mules for sale. The Abyssinians begin to salivate immediately: perhaps the white man doesn't know the right price and can be swindled. A train of mules would come to the hotel, some of them are really good, but terribly expensive. When this wave subsides, another starts: they bring sick mules, injured ones, ones with broken legs, in hope that the white man doesn't know anything about them; and only after all this do they begin to bring good mules for a fair price. In this fashion, we were lucky to buy four mules in three days. Abdoulaye helped us very much with this, and although he took bribes from the sellers, he nevertheless tried very hard to keep our interests in mind. However, the unscrupulousness of our translator Haile was fully revealed during these days. Not only did he not search for mules, but apparently he even made a deal with the innkeeper to detain us there for as long as possible. I dismissed him there on the spot in Harar.

I was advised to look for another translator in the Catholic mission. I went there with Iohandjian. We entered a half-open door and found ourselves in a large, impeccably clean courtyard. With tall white walls in the background, quiet Capuchin monks in brown vestments exchanged bows with us. Nothing reminded us of Abyssinia here, and it seemed like we were in Toulouse or Arles. In the simply furnished room monsieur himself, the bishop of Galla, a fifty-year-old Frenchman with eyes wide open, as if he were surprised, literally ran out to meet us. He was perfectly courteous and pleasant in talking to people, but you could clearly sense that the years spent among the savages, along with a general monastic naiveté, affected his life. In somewhat too light of a manner, like a seventeen-year-old boarding school girl, he was surprised, rejoiced and grieved at everything we told him. He knew one translator, it was a Galla by the name of Paul, a former pupil at the mission and a very good boy. He promised to send him to me. We said good-bye and returned to the hotel where Paul came two hours later. A tall fellow with a rather coarse peasant face, he readily smoked and drank even more readily, and at the same time he looked sleepy, moved limply, like a winter fly. We couldn't agree on a rate of pay. Later in Dire Dawa, I hired another mission pupil named Felix. According to the general opinion of all the Europeans who saw him, he looked like he was about to vomit. When he climbed stairs, you felt like lending him a hand. However, he was absolutely healthy and also *un tres brave garçon*, as the missioners observed. I was told that all pupils of the Catholic missions were like that. They give up their natural vitality and cleverness in exchange for dubious moral virtues.

In the evening, we went to a theater. The Dejazmach Tafari once saw performances of a touring Indian troupe in Dire Dawa and was so impressed that he decided to provide the same spectacle for his wife no matter what. The Indians, on his account, went to Harar, received living accommodations free of charge, and made themselves perfectly at home. It was the first theater in Abyssinia and it had immense success. With difficulty, we managed to find two seats in the front row, for which we had to move two respected Arabs to chairs that were added. The theater building turned out to be simply a fairground show booth: a low tin roof, unpainted walls, a dirt floor—all this was, perhaps, even beyond poor. The play was complex. Some Indian king in a cheap, loudly luxuriant costume was infatuated with a beautiful concubine and neglected not only his lawful spouse and his handsome young son, the prince, but also state affairs. The concubine, the Indian Phaedra, tried to seduce the prince, and in despair over her failure, slandered him in front of the king. The prince was exiled, and the king began to spend all his time drinking and in sensual pleasures. When enemies attacked, he did not defend his kingdom, in spite of the persuasions of his trusted warriors, and fled to survive. A new king entered the city. While hunting, by accident he saved the lawful wife of the former king (who had followed her son into exile) from robbers. He wanted to marry her, but when she refused, he told her that he agrees to treat her as his own mother. The new king had a daughter, and a fiancé had to be chosen for her. For that purpose, all the princes from surrounding lands gathered at the palace. The one who could shoot from an enchanted bow would be the chosen one. The exiled prince, dressed as a pauper, also came for the competition. Of course, only he could draw the bow and everyone was delighted to find out that he was of royal blood. The king gave him the throne with the hand of his daughter. The former king, who repented his errors, also returned and refused his rights to the throne in favor of the prince.

The only director's trick consisted of the fact that, when the curtain depicting a street of a large eastern city descended, actors dressed as inhabitants of that city played amusing little scenes that only remotely related to the general storyline of the play

The sets—alas!—were executed in a very bad European style, with the pretense of prettiness and realism. The most interesting thing was that all the roles were played by men. It might seem strange, but it did not harm the impression of the audience, but to the contrary, made the play stronger. The result was a pleasant unity of voices and movements so rarely found in our theaters. The actor who played the concubine was especially good, his face whitened and rouged, with a beautiful gypsy profile, he expressed so much passion and cat-like grace in the scene of the temptation of the king that the spectators were genuinely aroused. The eyes of the Arabs, who overcrowded the theater, especially flared up at the spectacle.

We returned to Dire Dawa, picked up all our luggage and new *askirs*, and in three days, we were already on the way back. We spent the night halfway along our ascent, and that was our first night in a tent. There was room there for only two of our beds and two suitcases of the Grum-Grizhmailo type,[79] placed one on top of the other between the beds, serving as a night table. A lantern, which had not been used before, spread its stench. For our dinner, we had *kita* (flour mixed with water and fried on a pan, which is the usual food here on a trip) and boiled rice, which we ate first with salt, and then with sugar. In the morning, we got up at six o'clock and continued on our way.

We were told that our friend, the Turkish consul, was in a hotel, a two-hour ride from Harar, and expected the Harar authorities to be officially

---

79 A reference to a kind of a rucksack used by a famous Russian geographer and zoologist, explorer of Western China, the Pamir, and the Tian Shan mountains, Grigory Grumm-Grzhimailo (1860-1936).

informed about his arrival. The German ambassador in Addis Ababa made an inquiry about this. We decided to drop by this hotel, having sent the caravan ahead.

Although the consul had not come in the execution of his duties, he had already begun receiving numerous Muslims, who saw in him a deputy of the Sultan himself and wished to greet him. According to local custom, everybody came with presents. Turkish gardeners brought vegetables and fruit, Arabs—lambs and chicken. Chiefs of the semi-independent Somali tribes sent their people to ask what he wanted—a lion, an elephant, a herd of horses, or a dozen ostrich skins with all the feathers intact. And only the Syrians, dressed in jackets and pretending to be Europeans, came in an uncouth manner and empty handed.

We spent about an hour with the consul, and when we came to Harar, we received unpleasant news that all our rifles and cartridges had been detained at customs. The next morning, our acquaintance, the Armenian merchant from the Harar environs, dropped in to pick us up to go together to meet the consul, who had finally received the necessary papers and was able to carry out a formal entrance to Harar. My companion was too tired from the day before, and I went alone. The road had a festive appearance. Arabs in white and colorful clothes were sitting around on the cliffs in reverent poses. Abyssinian *askirs* were scurrying about here and there. They were sent by the governor to provide for the honorary convoy and to keep order. The whites, that is the Greeks, Armenians, Syrians, and Turks, who all knew each other, were riding in groups, chatting and borrowing cigarettes from each other. Peasant Gallas, whom we had come across on our way, stepped aside in dismay upon seeing such festivities.

The consul, it seems I have forgotten to note that he was the consul-general, looked sufficiently majestic in his full dress uniform, richly embroidered with gold, a bright green ribbon across his shoulder, and a bright red fez. He mounted a big white horse, selected from among the most timid ones (he wasn't a good rider). Two *askirs* took the horse by the bridle, and we set off back to Harar. My place happened to be at the consul's right hand, to the left of him Callile Galeb was riding. He was the local representative of the merchant house of the Galebs. The governor's *askirs* were running in front, the Europeans were riding behind, and still farther behind them the devoted Muslims and various idling people were running. There were almost six hundred people in total. Greeks and Armenians, who rode behind us, pressed behind us mercilessly, each of them trying to demonstrate his closeness to the consul. Once his horse even decided to kick, but even that didn't stop these social climbers. Some dog created a big commotion when it decided to run and bark among the crowd. It was chased away and beaten, but it kept on. I moved away from the procession because the part of the stirrups that held the saddle had broken, and I returned to the hotel with my two *askirs*. The next day, in accordance with the invitation received the day before and confirmed today, we moved from the hotel to the Turkish consulate.

In order to travel through Abyssinia, you must have a pass from the government. I sent a wire about this to the Russian attorney in charge of these things in Addis Ababa and received an answer that the order to issue a pass for me had been sent to the head of Harar customs, Nagadras Bistrati. However, the Nagadras announced that he could do nothing without his superior, Dejazmach Tafari. We had to bring a present to the Dejazmach. When we were sitting at the Dejazmach's, two strong Negroes brought in a case of vermouth, which I had bought for him, and placed it at his feet. It was done on the advice of Kalil Galeb, who was also the person designated to introduce us. The Dejazmach's palace was a large two-story wooden building with a painted porch, overlooking an inner, quite dirty courtyard. The building resembled a fairly run-down dacha, a summer place, somewhere in Pargolovo or Terioki.[80] A few dozen *askirs* were hanging around in the courtyard, behaving rather arrogantly. We ascended the stairs and, after momentarily waiting on the porch, entered a large room, all covered with carpets, the entire furniture of which consisted of a few chairs and a velvet armchair for the Dejazmach. The Dejazmach got up to meet us and shook our hands. He was dressed in a *shamma*, like all Abyssinians. Looking at his chiseled face, framed by a black, wavy goatee, at his large, gazelle-like, dignified eyes, and at his entire bearing, one could guess that he was a prince. That was not surprising: he was a son of the Ras Makonnen, who was a cousin and a friend of the emperor Menelik, and thus traced his origin directly to King Solomon and the Queen of Sheba. We asked him about the pass, but in spite of the gift, he answered that without an order from Addis Ababa, he could do nothing. Unfortunately, we couldn't even get an authorization from the Nagadras that the order had been received, because the Nagadras went to look for a mule with the mail from Europe that had disappeared on the road from

---

80   Places near St Petersburg, popular for summer vacationing.

Dire Dawa to Harar. Then we asked the Dejazmach permission to take his picture, and he immediately agreed to that. In a few days, we came back with a camera. *Askirs* spread carpets right in the courtyard, and we took the picture of the Dejazmach in his blue ceremonial dress. Then it was his wife's, the princess's, turn.

She was a sister of the Liege Iyasu, the heir to the throne, and consequently, a granddaughter of Menelik. She was twenty-two, three years older than her husband, and the features of her face were very pleasant, in spite of a certain fullness, which had already spoiled her figure. Although, it seemed that she was expecting. The Dejazmach paid the most touching attention to her. He himself sat her in the required pose, straightened her dress, and asked us to take her picture several times in order that they would be sure it turned out. During that time, it was revealed that he spoke French but was shy to do so, thinking, not without reason, that it was unbecoming for a prince to make mistakes. We took the picture of the princess with her two girl servants.

We sent a new telegram to Addis Ababa and began our work in Harar. My companion began to collect insects in the city's environs. I accompanied him a couple of times. It was a wonderfully pleasant diversion for the soul: to wander along white paths among the coffee fields, to climb cliffs, to descend to the river, and to find tiny beauties everywhere—red, blue, green, and gold. My companion collected up to fifty of them a day while avoiding taking samples of the same ones. My work was completely different. I was collecting ethnographical items. Shamelessly, I stopped passers-by in order to examine the clothes they wore, entered houses without permission, and scrutinized the utensils, got carried away trying to obtain information about the purpose of some items from the Hararites, who didn't understand what this was all about. I was ridiculed when I bought old clothes. One market woman cursed me when I decided to take her picture, and some people refused to sell me what I requested, thinking that I needed it for sorcery. To obtain an item that was considered sacred here—a turban worn by the Hararites who visited Mecca—I had to feed its owner, an old half-witted sheik, for a whole day with *khat* leaves (a drug, consumed by Muslims). And in the house of Kavos' mother at the Turkish consulate, I scrounged in a stinking basket for old things, and found many interesting items there. This hunt for treasures is quite fascinating: little by little, a picture of the entire nation's life unfolds before your eyes, and the impatience to see more and more of it constantly grows. After I bought a spinning loom, I saw that I had to learn about the weaving loom as well. After I bought utensils, I had to obtain food samples. In total, I obtained about seventy pieces of purely Hararite items, avoiding buying Arabic and Abyssinian ones. However, all things must come to an end. We decided that Harar had been studied and explored as much as possible, and since we'll receive the pass only in about eight days, we decided to go to Jijjiga, to the Gabaratal Somali tribe, traveling light—only with one draught mule and three *askirs*. I'll allow myself to discuss this in a later chapter.

CHAPTER FOUR

Harar was established about nine hundred years ago by Muslim descendants from Tigre, who had escaped religious persecution, and by Arabs who intermixed with them. It is located on a small but extremely fertile plateau that borders on the north and on the west the Danakil dessert, on the east the land of Somali, and on the south the high wooded area of Meta; in total, the area that it occupies equals eighty square kilometers. The Hararites live only in town and work in gardens where they grow coffee and *khat* (a tree with intoxicating leaves); the rest of the area, covered with pasture lands and fields of *durra* and maize as early as the sixteenth century, was occupied by the Gallas and the Kotus, who are farmers. Harar was an independent state until 1875. That year, Negus Menelik in the battle at Chelonko in the Chercher mountains dealt a crushing defeat to the Harar Negus Abdullah and took him into captivity, where he soon died. His son now lives under government house arrest in Abyssinia and is nominally called the Harar Negus and receives a substantial pension. I saw him in Addis Ababa: he was a handsome, portly Arab with a pleasant stately face and manner of movement, but with a certain timidity in his eyes. However, he did not express any intentions to regain the throne for himself. After the victory, Menelik entrusted rule over Harar to his cousin Ras Makonnen, one of the greatest government leaders of Abyssinia. Through successful wars Makonnen expanded the boundaries of his province to the entire land of the Danakils and the greater part of the Somali Peninsula. After his death, his son Dejazmach Ilma ruled over Harar, but he died within a year. Then the new leader was Dejazmach Balcha. He was a strong and stern person, and people talk about him even today, some with indignation, some with genuine respect. When he arrived at Harar, there was a whole city block where cheerful women of the night lived. His soldiers started to quarrel over them, and sometimes it even led to murder. Balcha ordered all the women brought to the city square and had them sold at public auction [as slave women], making the condition that their buyers watch over the behavior of their new women slaves. If even one of them was observed continuing work in her former trade, then she would be executed, and the accomplice in her crime would have to pay a fine of ten *thalers*. Now Harar is nearly the most virtuous city in the world because the Hararites did not properly understand their prince and carried his order to include common adultery as well. When the mail from Europe failed to arrive, Balcha ordered all the inhabitants of the house in which the empty bag was found to be hanged, and fourteen corpses dangled for a long time from the trees along the road between Dire Dawa and Harar. He refused to pay taxes to the Negus, maintaining that on that side of Awash, he was the Negus, and proposed removing the other Negus from his governorship. He knew that he was valued as the only skillful strategist in Abyssinia. Now he is a governor in a remote area of Sidamo and conducts himself there as he did in Harar.

The Dejazmach Tafari, to the contrary, is soft, indecisive, and not enterprising. Order is maintained only by the lieutenant governor Fitaurari Gabre, an old dignitary of the Balchi school. The latter eagerly gives twenty or thirty "giraffes," that is, lashes with a whip made out of giraffe's skin and even hangs people sometimes, but very rarely.

The Europeans, the Abyssinians, and the Gallas, as though in agreement, hate the Haratites. The Europeans hate them for their treachery and venality, the Abyssinians—for their laziness and weakness. The Gallas' hatred is the result of many centuries of fighting and has almost mystical overtones. "The son of angels, who goes shirtless (that is, Gallas) is not supposed to enter the houses of black Hararites"—is sung by them, and they usually fulfill this testament. All of this does not seem quite justified to me. It is true that the Hararites inherited the most repulsive qualities of the Semitic race, but no more than the Arabs of Cairo or Alexandria, and it is their misfortune that they have to live among the knightly Abyssinians, the work-loving Gallas, and the noble Arabs of Yemen. They are very well-read, know the Koran and Arabic literature perfectly, but are not distinguished by any particular religiosity. Their main saint is the Sheik Abukir, who came about two hundred years ago from Arabia and was buried in Harar. Numerous platan trees, so called *aulia*, in the city and its environs are dedicated to him. Local Muslims call *aulia* everything that possesses the power to perform miracles for the glory of Allah. There are *aulia* corpses and living people, trees and items. For example, in the market in Ginir, a merchant refused to sell me a locally produced umbrella for a long time, saying that it was *aulia*. However, more educated people know that an inanimate object cannot be sacred by itself and that the miracles are performed by the spirit of that or another saint who lives inside this item.

AFRICAN DIARY 2

[The description of the second diary of N. Gumilev is from V. Brunguleev's book *In the Midst of Earthly Travel. A Documentary Tale of the Life and Work of Nikolai Gumilev. Years: 1886-1913*. Only two thin notebooks remain from the diary, without covers, ten-and-a-half by seventeen-and-a-half centimeters in size, stapled with thin metal staples. The text is written with black ink and in general on one side of the pages and only the last pages – in pencil. The paper is somewhat deteriorated. It is also soiled and burned on the edges. Besides episodes of travel, there are descriptions of items from the ethnographic collection collected in Harar on May 30th and 31st, 1915, small sketches, occasional travel notes, and the first draft of a sonnet, later published in the journal Neva, under the title "Desdemona."

The diary describes events from June 17 to August 3, 1913, and for all the notes, there is only one date marking the 31st day of travel, but it allowed a certain approximation to date other days, which are marked simply by ordinal numbers.

Since the diary was in the possession of Gumilev's second wife Anna Engelgardt, it apparently was not known to his relatives, and it is doubtful that the poet gave it to anyone to read, since the short and unpolished notes could not generate much interest at that time. The scenes described in this diary were known probably from the stories of "little" Kolya. Remembering the stories many years later, Gumilev's sister-in-law, the mother of little Kolya, still could remember something from them, recorded what she knew, and gave these notes to Olga N. Vysotsky.

The following are the notes from Gumilev's second diary.

Number 1.

We left at twelve through the Towam Gates.

We stopped by the house of the Nagadras, on the invitation of our boy translator. We went in to say good-bye, then Abdulai ran away and we went to Gorikian's land. We spent the night having eaten chicken and *kita* in the Provence oil, which was marvelous.

Judging by the following entries, the travelers first went along the familiar road to Dire Dawa.

Number 2.

We left at eleven. In the morning, Kolya collected many insects. The road went straight to the west, the same that led to Dire-Dawa. Many cracks in the rain time of rivers [? –VB].

At first the road was almost red. Then there was the River Amaressa, Lakes Aramaia and Adeli, both salt-water. A curious prohibition against shooting birds. The mule is limping, so almost all the time I needed to walk. On both sides there were maize fields and molachi hedges. Grass was sown here and there.

Number 3.

We left at ten, stopped at five. The first half of the day trip was to the south, the second – to the west. In the middle of the journey we saw Gara Muletta[81] to the north, about fifteen kilometers from us. We made our way through the molachi thicket, cutting them. The road was littered with thorns in many places. The land was *degga* – groves of tree-like molachi, occasional *durro* fields. We stopped by the River Woter (a creek) at the foot of Golla Mountain, killed a duck, at night we shot at hyenas. The country is called Metta, with one thousand warriors under the leadership of Kenyazmach Walde-Marriam Abainech.

Number 4.

Forests begin; we passed Golla Mountain and stooped at the mountain Weldiya: a quarrel with the Garizmach Kailu and a judge.

[*During the next two days (entries 5 and 6) the party went southwest, crossing many valleys and buttes that were completely covered with forests.*]

---

81   A mountain peak in East Harerghe, Oromiya, Ethiopia.

Number 7.

We visited Garizmach's wife; a dinner in the tent of an Englishman, a chat; a Russian doctor; a child and a stepdaughter (from the brothers Grimm's fairy tales).

Number 8

We walked for six hours to the south; a gently sloping descent to Apia; a path went between a range of low hills; thorns and mimosas; strange flowers: one as if it were mad with its petals thrown back and its stamens sticking out; we became separated from the caravan and decided to go to the town. We were going up under cliffs for an hour-and-a-half; a sleepy town; we met the vice-governor who took us to the caravan and drank tea with us, sitting on the floor.

The town was established about thirty years ago by the Abyssinians. It is called Ganami ("*Utrenitb*" in Galla, that is, "the good one"). The head of the region or the area, Fitaurari Asfau, lives in it with one thousand soldiers of the garrison. There are about a hundred houses in it. The Church of St. Michael; strange stones with holes in them, piled one on top of another, there are even sometimes three, one on top of another. Some recall a little fort with an embrasure, others – a sphinx, the third – Cyclonic structures. Here we saw a curious trap for a porcupine ("jart"). It comes at night to eat *durro*, and the Abyssinians set out a kind of a telegraph wire or butler's bell-rope, one end of which is in the house, and a wooden dish and empty gourds are hung on the other end. At night they pull the wire, and it makes noise in the field, and the *jart* runs away. A day's trip away to the south there are lions, in two days' – rhinoceros.

[*Most likely the travelers spent the night in town. The next day they failed to leave early and had to travel during the hottest part of the day. The terrain started to go downward, and the caravan entered the kola, which forms the left bank of a large river, the Webe.*

Number 9.

We left at twelve noon. A long but easy descent. We see villages more and more seldom. The *barha* (the desert – SY) and *kola* (lowland – SY) began. Tall molachi and mimosas. A wild cat, a turkey and a leopard. Pass the water and stop in the desert at five o'clock. The customs office was in a small village that we passed. The officials ran after us and didn't want to accept our permission to pass, demanding the following from the Magadras Bifati. "The dog doesn't know the master of its master." We chased them away.

[*The movement across the desert was especially difficult. Water could be found very rarely. The trail often disappeared. During one of treks the* askirs *were at the point of mutiny. Gumilev had to promise them additional rations while they travelled across the* barha. *At night they did not set up tents and slept right on the stony ground. Meanwhile there were a lot of scorpions and, of course, poisonous snakes.*]

Number 10.

We left at six. Terrible heat. The *askirs* are ready to revolt. I quieted them down with the promise to feed them in the desert. Our path goes through thorns. We've lost our way. The night was spent without water and a tent. Fear of scorpions.

Number 11.

We left at six o'clock. Walked without any road. In two hours we found a basin with running water. By eleven o'clock we dispersed to look for the road. Only thorns, but finally the agreed-upon rifle shot. We came to a Gallasian village, asked them to sell us milk but were told they didn't have any. At that time Abyssinians approached (two horsemen with five servants – the *askirs* of Atto Nado, who asked if they could go to Ganami with us). They immediately went to the village, entered the houses, and procured milk. We drank and paid them. Old Gallasian women were charmed. The Abyssinians didn't drink; it was Friday. They did it for us and, looking for us by our tracks, came to these slums. We didn't know the road and grabbed a Galla for him to take us there. At that time terrible, semi-naked, threatening men came running in from the pastures, one of them especially looked like a Stone Age man. We argued with them for a long time, but finally after they found out that we paid for everything, they went to see us off and in the road, having received some *bakshish* from me, thanked me, and we parted as friends.

We stopped at four o'clock by the water. An incident took place in the evening. The day before our burnoose disappeared and according the

Abyssinian custom my *askirs* had to pay for it, but they looked through all their things and finally started to look through the things of the Shangal *askir*, who had strayed away from his master's, the Nagodi, and had joined us on the way. He came to complain to us about it and suggested to take the case to a judge. He logically pointed out that there were no judges in the *barha*, and while some were holding him, others cut his bag open. The first thing there was our burnoose. The thief tried to escape, but he was caught and tied up. Our friends the Abyssinians, who came in, loaned us shackles, and the thief was put in irons. Then he announced that six thallers had been stolen from him. I was supposed to pay, and I announced that I distributed this money among my *askirs*. Then the thief was searched, and money was found in his cape. It outraged everyone.

[*The next day the trip began very early. After traveling for five hours, the caravan approached a small village, the name of which was omitted by Gumilev. There they bought some provisions and utensils and moved on.*]

Number 12.

Left at six. By eleven o'clock, we bought oil from the head of the village. Bought a milk-pail.

Calves and baby camels live in the house. Then we couldn't find water for a long time and walked till four four thirty, altogether ten hours. We were terribly tired. Took a swim in a basin, an *arshin*[82] deep. Fell asleep on the stones without a tent. It was raining at night, and we all got soaked.

[*The badly spent night had its effect on the length of the trek next day. It was short. During the day the travelers hunted for their zoological collection and in the evening developed their photographs made the day before.*]

Number 13.

Walked for an hour-and-a-half, then the Abyssinians shot an antelope, and it took us a long time to skin it. Kite birds and condors came flying. We killed four and skinned two of them. I took a shot at a crow. Bullets bounce off its feathers. The Abyssinians say that it is a sacred bird. In the evening we developed our photographs.

---

82   *Arshin* is an old Russian linear measure, equal to about 50 cm.

Number 14.

The Abyssinians lost their mules and went to look for them. My *askirs* demanded that we wait for them, because only they knew the road. I agreed to wait until twelve, and we left during the terrible heat. Walked 'till five.

The *barha* looked like a fruit garden. Here it became lighter and not as thick. We stopped by a village, near the entrance. To prevent cows from rushing all at once through the gates, a large pit was dug out in front of them. We entered the village that consisted of only six straw huts (women and children wear pieces of leather instead of clothes.) Visited the school. Bought a spoon and tar for ink. The teacher was a terrible swindler. He studied with the Somalis. Children were on vacation because of the cattle plague.

For the first time I saw a prayer to Sheik Nura-Ukeino.

Number 15.

In the morning, the professor (*Gumilev most likely means the teacher here* – SY) received a shirt so that he could show us the way, but for a long time he tried to run away from us so we caught him and beat him up. The Abyssinians caught up with us. We walked for four hours and stopped without water or setting up a tent.

[*The expedition was descending for eight days along the slope toward the valley of the river Wabi. Here at its widest part the river is joined by many tributaries flowing southward. One of these tributaries was the river Ramis.*]

Number 16.

We descend to the river Ramis, which begins in Metta and flows into the Wabi at that spot. We forded it and after a half- hour of a scenic route reached the Wabi, which was flooded. We shouted and shot in order to scare off crocodiles, then started to swim across. The crocodiles circled nearby and frightened the mules that began to drown and carried off by the current. A crocodile tore off a gaiter from Kolya, whose mule had toppled over. A second one bit another boy on the finger. Soaked, we climbed onto the shore and dried off there naked for a long time. Then we fished. We caught fifteen white and two black fish with whiskers. The fish were really biting.

By the evening, we had a difficult two-hour ascent. Slept in the desert without a tent.

[*The terrain along which the caravan continued to travel was still semi-desert with sparse vegetation and by its geographical conditions – a typical* kola. *The route most likely went to the south of the villages Gubbisa and Beltu through a very sparsely populated area.*]

Number 17.

Left at six and moved along till eleven to the west. There was nothing but the *barha*; met a giant Galla. They all are like that in Arusi. For money, he showed where water was and sold us oil. Our torment was over. We rested, drank the terrible, sour milk, left at four, and went kept going till half-past six. [*Unclear* VB] … of the mule. Slept in the tent.

Number 18.

Left at six and walked to the west for two hours, then killed an *ambaraille* (an antelope) and as usual, stopped to skin it and eat. A group of Gallas approached us – an old man with a boy and a young man with a child, who were supposed to be their *ashkirs*. We gave the back of the beast to the old man. Then we searched for insects, skinned two parrots.

Fasika was writing down a folktale.

Number 19.
We separated from the caravan in order to visit a village. There we haggled for a long time but didn't buy anything. On the way we saw hogs, killed the little one and skinned it. In the evening again traveled for a total of five hours.

[*On the twentieth day of the journey they saw a mountain on which the town of Sheikh Hussein was located. Gumilev decided to visit it, and the Abyssinians who travelled with him went straight to Ginir. For the next three days the caravan moved toward Sheikh Hussein. On the way there they did some hunting.*

They made a stop in one of the Galla towns. The inhabitants of it invited the travelers to what most likely was a wake because it took place at a cemetery. By evening Gumilev felt sick. He had a fever and kidney pain.]

Number 21.

We moved through a valley. A lot of game, killed a jackal. We stopped after three hours of walking because the Gallas killed two oxen at the cemetery and invited us to eat. In the evening we went hunting: killed a huge bird and saw a deer. I have a fever and kidney trouble.

Number 22.

We traveled for eight hours, carrying the rotten bird. Stopped before a town on the other side of the precipice.

Number 23.

We went to the town for three hours. Stopped at the outskirts under two molachais. Two Gallas came, who advised us to get rid of the others. Abba Mudha sent provisions. We went to him; he received us in a house with a flat roof where there were three rooms: one partitioned off with skins, another with clay. Utensils were piled up there. A donkey wanted to enter. Mudha imitates Abyssinian chiefs and gets a swelled head.

Then after a day of terrible heat, we went to examine the tomb of Sheik Hussein. This is a cemetery fenced off with a tall stone wall with the small stone house of the door-keeper from Jimma outside. We took off our shoes; stones pricked our feet. Houses (*by houses Gumilev means tombs or mausoleums* – SY) are whitewashed on the outside but not plastered inside. The best house was the round tomb of Sheik Hussein. Then there were tombs of his son, his daughter, Sheik Busher (the son of Sheik Mohammed), Sheik Abdul-Kadir, and some noble Gallas. In the evening we worked on writing the history of Sheik Hussein with Hadji Abdul-Medjid and Kabir Abass.

In the morning we went to watch the place of miracles in the precipice. We saw the cave where he lived and in the cave – a pregnant woman, a snake, and the sanctuary. Then we saw two other caves. In the second we saw holes through which only the sinless can crawl. Both Abba Mudha and I crawled through.

Then we saw the stone on the bottom of the precipice where Sheik Hussein prayed when his favorite pupil came to him and flew down from a height of forty *sazhens*;[83] then after a deep sleep we photographed the book and the town.

Number 25.

We left at eleven. At three o'clock, we came upon a watering hole for cows but didn't stop, and then we found out that there wouldn't be water for a long time and we kept going till eight o'clock, that is, till *degga*.
The last hour was an ascent into darkness.
We didn't eat anything since morning. Everybody is sick. Our path is to the southwest. The weather is cloudy. There is no rain.

Number 26.

We traveled for four hours. Stopped in the village to buy milk. Examined the huts. We bought a machine for cleaning cotton. [*The number 12 is written after this word in the text. - VB*] Then an old Abyssinian came with his son. This village [unclear] is given to him. Then he took us to his place and covering us with the flap of his dress to ward off the evil eye, gave us milk to drink. We stopped to feed our mules. Searched for gold in the river.

Number 27.

Moved along for ten hours to Ghinir. The place is desolate, it is *degga*. We stopped ouside the town: Fasiki — a friend — in charge of the market; we dined in the house of two Syrians from the house of Galeb.

Number 28.

We are resting and buying provisions. In the evening, Fasika and I, returning from the town, lost our way. I asked Wakkine about Wolaga.[84]

---

83   *Sazhen* is an old Russian linear measure equal to about 2.1 meters.
84   Wakkine was the name of one of Gumilev's *ashkirs*. Wolaga is probably one of the Ethiopian provinces, the right spelling of which is Wolega. However, Gumilev's interest in this region seems strange since it was located very far away from the route of his expedition.

[*The travelers spent two days in Ginir. The entries for these days are marked 29 and 30. It is clear from them that the travelers spent these days buying various items for their collection and also some provisions. They made acquaintance with some Greeks and invited them to dinner at their place. They ordered flour to be ground for them and made other preparations before continuing on their journey.*

The expedition left Ginir on the 4th (17th) of July. This is the only date (as it was pointed out earlier) put in the diary on the thirty first day of travel.]

Number 31.

17th/ 4th of July. We've been moving for six hours to the west. In the south a mountain range separates us from Gabba;[85] a gloomy *degga*, a lot of jackals.

Number 32.

We've been going for four hours because Fasika is sick; stopped in a hollow. Ate a couple ducks.

Number 33.

We've been moving along for four hours descending to Wabi; on the way we tried to catch a rat; there are Abyssinian settlements everywhere, a bazaar without a village; a chief in a booth,[86] an announcement about an escaped slave; beauties; a woman with a goiter; we bought a clay and wicker vase for oil.

Number 34.

Descended to the Wabi for four hours. Crossing, rain, problems with mules; paid four *thalers*, went for an hour from the water looking for grass.

---

85   Gabba was the administrative center of the Bale province. It was located on the edge of the famous national park of Ethiopia - the Bale-Mautince, in which one of the highest mountains, Batu (4,310 m), is located.
86   A reference to an Abyssinian custom of a high official (often called a judge), who oversaw the working of a market place from a small cabin placed on the top of a pole.

Number 35.

We got up at two o'clock at night in order to leave the *kola* before the heat. Went along for six hours and stopped to rest. Then went from three to five; ascent into the *degga* [unclear - VB]. Stopped by the Abyssinian town under construction. We got milk from a Galla in exchange for salt.

Number 36.

We've been going for five hours along the *degga*. There are very few villages. There is no firewood. During the day it was drizzling from one to three. At night it was pouring. In the village they prepared [unclear]. Fasika killed a duck that I roasted.

Number 37.

We've been going for five hours to the northeast; killed two ducks; took many pictures in the village; on the side is the servant of Sh[eik] H[ussein].

Number 38.

We moved along for five hours. To the east is the town [unclear - VB] Kubbada; Ticho is in the mountains. Many [unclear - VB]. In the evening, an ox came and licked the donkey. Ibrahim says that the owner of the ox will die; Mohammed says that oxen like sweat.

Number 39.

We've been going for six hours. Stopped in an empty village, the inhabitants moved away to the *kola* for the rainy season because there is too much mud and oxen drown in it. Wakkine is sick; we sleep in the house.

Number 40.

We are staying put because Wakkine is sick. We saw a Galla farmer. Went to get *medafels* (wild goats). There were a lot of them but they did not let us approach. I wounded one and we chased it for two hours. It started to rain. We hid in the burnoose of a Galla. A revolver disappeared.

Number 41.

Went for five hours along the *degga*. There are a lot of abandoned villages. In one of them we waited sitting on a bed for the rain to stop. A two-hour descent into the *Woina-degga*.[87] We could see Ita already.

Number 42.

After three hours of the charming road with baboons and [unclear - VB] tent; the white Mr. Rey comes out of it. We sit down and decide to spend the night so that tomorrow we pass together through customs. He has horses; I have the permission. In the evening he was brought food from the wife of Atto-Mandafra. We eat together. The mule coughs.

Number 43. In the morning

Number 49. We approach the monk.

Number 50. We are sitting with the monk.

Number 51. We leave the monk.

Number 52. We entered Largohardam.

Number 53. The road (? - VB)

---

87   (literally "grape zone"; woina — from Greek *oinos*, wine), the central belt of the Ethiopian plateau, Many of the most important crops are native to the savannas of the Woina Dega belt — grasses (wheat, barley, and millet) as well as flax, peas, and other crops. The Woina Dega is the most heavily populated belt of the Ethiopian plateau. Grains, including corn and local types of grasses such as *teff* and *raggee*, are grown, as well as tobacco, oil-producing plants, citrus fruits, and grapes.

UNDER THE UNNECESSARY NET OF LONGITUDES AND LATITUDES: THE PROBLEM OF THE RELATIONSHIP BETWEEN MAN AND SPACE IN NIKOLAI GUMILEV'S AFRICAN PHOTOGRAPHS

Africa occupied a very special place for Nikolai Gumilev. During his lifetime, he made four trips to the North and East Africa, the most extensive of them a trip to Abyssinia in 1913. That trip was made on assignment and on account of the Museum of Ethnography and Anthropology of the Russian Academy of Science in St. Petersburg, which commissioned Gumilev to gather ethnographic materials in that region.

In addition to physical cultural artifacts, Gumilev returned with more than 200 photographs from the trip, taken mostly by his nephew Nikolai Sverchkov, nicknamed Little Kolya, but under the supervision of and with the direct participation of Big Kolya (Gumilev himself), who played a significant role in the process.

The photographic equipment that they used created photographs on glass plates with the use of silver emulsion. The equipment was quite heavy, consisting of a wooden folding camera for plates of up to 20" x 24" in size, bottles with chemicals, and other supplies for developing the photos. In addition to these items, travelers had to carry bulky boxes with sheets of glass. Stories from the expeditions included accounts of constant problems in transporting this fragile cargo, and Gumilev's expedition was not an exception by any means (consider, for example, the story about crossing the Wabi River in a funicular).

To some extent, Gumilev was a typical European traveler to the Orient: one of those adventurers who, from the moment of photography's invention in the middle of the 19th century, traveled all over the world with their cameras and brought back thousands of photographs. As John Berger writes in his book *Another Way of Telling*:

> ...all over the world during the nineteenth century, European travelers, soldiers, colonial administrators, adventurers, took photographs of "the natives," their customs, their architecture, their richness, their poverty, their women's breasts, their headdresses; and these images, besides provoking amazement, were presented and read as proof of the justice of the imperial division of the world. The division between those who organized and rationalized and surveyed, and those who *were* surveyed.[1]

Contemporary photography theorists consider photography (especially the early ethnographic photography) to be a means of and a reflection of the European domination over ingenious populations and appropriation of their living space: According to Alan Thomas, "As a symbol of Western technology and an instrument of its expanding world vision, the camera accompanied expeditions which carried the Western presence into remote or unexplored territories."[2] Distant, mysterious places that were of little interest up to that point became strangely attractive with the emergence of photography. Photographs packed in glass plates and brought back to London or Paris to be reproduced in numerous copies could be displayed in handsome albums in the drawing rooms of the wealthy. Susan Sonntag observes that "[b]ringing the exotic near, rendering the familial and homely exotic, photographs make the entire world available as an object of appraisal."[3] Thus, the frightening, wild, and exotic places were rendered domestic, familiar. They became the property of a middle-class man.

For Gumilev, as for other travelers to the Orient, photography was also a way of mastering the indigenous space. However, his end goal was different: it was not to dominate and appropriate that space, but to translate the physical reality of "longitudes and latitudes" into the mythic landscape of Acmeist poetry. This translation was made, no matter how paradoxically it sounds, through the poet's merging with African space through his poems and photographs.

---

1   John Berger and John Mohr, *Another Way of Telling* (New York: Pantheon Books, 1982), p. 97.
2   Alan Thomas, *Time in a Frame. Photography and the Nineteenth-Century Mind* (New York: Schocken Books, 1977), p. 12.
3   Susan Sontag, *On Photography* (New York: Farrar, Straus and Giroux, 1977), p. 110.

In this respect, it is necessary to consider Gumilev's interest in photography in the context of Acmeist poetry. When Gumilev proclaimed the emergence of Acmeism, it signified the restoration of the material, tangible world in poetry. "Comparing Acmeism with the preceding artistic movement in his manifesto article "The Heritage of Symbolism and Acmeism," Gumilev pointed out the material saturation of the verbal composition of Acmeist poetry: "For us, the hierarchy in the realm of phenomena is only the specific gravity of each of them, and with that the gravity of the most insignificant of them is nevertheless incommensurably greater than the absence of weight, of non-existence."[4] Contemporary photography theorists point out that photography, being itself an object, a real thing, creates an independent physical reality because it transforms the world from existing "out there" to existing "inside" a photograph. In Halla Beloff's words, "[s]uch is the power of camera that we can easily think of photographs as having a kind of independent reality."[5] In a photograph, a person is placed in particular spatial relations that reveal hidden, concealed meanings of objects. For the photographer Carthiert-Bresson, to take a photograph meant "'to find the structure of the world - to revel in the pure pleasure of form,' to disclose that 'in all this chaos, there is order.'"[6]

Roland Barthes goes even further, maintaining that photography is, in fact, a living organism: "Photography... is nevertheless mortal: as a living organism it is born on the level of sprouting silver grains, blossoms for a moment, then ages... Under the influence of light and moisture it fades out, weakens, disappears."[7] This "living process" of photography is perfectly exemplified in photographs taken by Gumilev and Sverchkov during the 1913 expedition. These photographs were made in field conditions and then spent more than seventy-five years in a storage room of the Museum of Ethnography and Anthropology in St. Petersburg. As a result of deterioration and decomposition of the silver emulsion, a new landscape, "executed" in silvery hues, with grainy texture, emerges on Gumilev's original photograph of the Abyssinian forest.

---

4   Nikolai Gumilev, *Sobranie sochinenii v trekh tomakh*, v. 3 (Moscow: Xudozh. literatura, 1991), p. 18.
5   Halla Beloff, *Camera Culture* (Oxford: Basil Blackwell, 1985), p. 15.
6   As quoted in Susan Sontag, *On Photography* (New York: Farrar, Straus and Giroux, 1977), p. 100.
7   Roland Barthes, *Camera Lucida. Reflections on Photography* (New York: Hill and Wang, 1981), p. 93.

This also makes an interesting connection with cabal and magic, in which Gumilev was very much interested. Barthes writes: "And if Photography belongs to the world in its residual sensitivity in relation to myth, we have to rejoice to the richness of symbolism: the beloved body is immortalized by means of the precious metal - the silver (a monument and luxury); to which we can add the notion that this metal like all metals of Alchemy is alive."[8] In connection with this, we can say that photography is not simply a recording of reality, but a revelation of the essence of an object or a person that establishes this essence forever in the living metal, thus imparting it with immortality. This also explains why neither lithographs, nor sketches, nor stories, nor artifacts brought by travelers from their trips could compare with photographs in the power of representing the living truth. An alien, exotic life, caught at a certain moment, is revealed to the viewer upon the first glance at a photograph. Thus it comes as no surprise that in Gumilev's descriptions of his activities in collecting ethnographic materials, taking pictures of people, of their clothes, customs, etc. occupies the same place as acquiring the actual objects:

> My work was completely different. I was collecting ethnographic items. Shamelessly, I stopped passers-by in order to examine the clothes they wore, entered houses without permission, and scrutinized the utensils, lost my head trying to obtain information about the purpose of some item from the Hararites who didn't understand what this was all about. I was ridiculed when I bought old clothes, one market woman cursed me when I decided to take her picture, and some people refused to sell me what I requested, thinking that I needed it for my witchery.[9]

I would like to point out two things in the quoted passage: the perception of photography as witchery and the process of reconstructing the life and culture of a certain people through direct contact with physical objects of their culture. It must also be noted that both objects and photographs are perceived as categories of the same significance.

---

8   *Ibid.*, p. 81.
9   N. Gumilev, "Afrikanskii dnevnik," in Nikolai Gumilev, *Sobranie sochinenii v trekh tomakh*, v. 3 (Moscow: Xudozh. literatura, 1991), p. 279.

Among almost two hundred and fifty photographs that were made during the 1913 expedition, there are several, in my opinion, that in particular express the nature of the African space and the relationships between this space and man (both the Europeans as well as those native to Africa) in the most complete and profound manner. Unlike the majority of his contemporaries traveling to the Orient from Western Europe, Gumilev succeeded in stepping on the threshold of interaction with the reality he photographed, creating a new, disappearing space between him and what he photographed.

Let's consider several portrait photographs first, starting with the portrait of Dejazmach[10] Tafari, the original title and name of the future last Emperor of Ethiopia Haile Sellassie. Here is how Gumilev describes the meeting with Tafari:

> The Dejazmach got up to meet us and shook our hands. He was dressed in a *shamma*, like all Abyssinians. By looking at his chiseled face, bordered with a black, wavy goatee, by his big gazelle-like dignified eyes, and by his entire bearing, one could guess that he was a prince. That was not surprising, he was a son of the Ras Makonnen, who was a cousin and a friend of the emperor Mennelik, and traced his origin directly to King Solomon and the Queen of Sheba.

Gumilev creates a verbal portrait of the Abyssinian aristocrat, using vivid visual imagery for this purpose. It is important to note that Gumilev perceives the Dejazmach first of all as a prince, placing him in an historical, even legendary, context. In his photograph of the prince, Gumilev wanted to stress precisely this aspect:

> Then we asked the Dejazmach permission to take his picture and he immediately agreed to that. In a few days we came back with a camera. Ashkers spread carpets right in the courtyard, and we took the picture of the Dejazmach in his blue ceremonial dress.

As we can see from the description of the photographic process, special conditions were arranged for it: the person was photographed in

---

10   Dejazmach was an Ethiopian military title meaning commander of the vanguard or general of the gate. Ashkers in the description that follows are servants.

a ceremonial dress and in a space created specifically for photographing. The ceremonial dress reflects the perception of the photographed as a prince. It is also interesting to point out that it is only from Gumilev himself that we find out that the dress was blue, since the black and white photograph gives no indication of colors or of it being a ceremonial dress. In other words, the concrete historical context is given in extrinsic (that is, not internally characteristic of the representation) forms, and our perception of the photograph takes a totally different route, close to one offered by Roland Barthes: "Photography turned a subject into an object, one can even say, a museum object... In front of the lens I am simultaneously the one who thinks that I am; the one who I want others to think that I am; the one who the photographer thinks that I am: and the one who he uses to demonstrate his art."[11] Except for the last statement (I do not think that Sverchkov or Gumilev thought of their photographs as art works), Barthes' statement can be fully applied to the photographic portrait of Tafari. Our historical knowledge adds a few more aspects to the perception of the Dejazmach's photograph. During the last few years of the rule of the great Ethiopian Emperor Menelik II, the influence of French culture was quite strong. Tafari's gesture represents, in some respect, the reverse gesture of Napoleon's famous gesture in placing his right hand inside his jacket. On the photograph, the future Emperor sticks his hand out from under his ceremonial dress. The gesture establishes (no matter how slight) a semantic connection between these two rulers, based on opposite vectors. Napoleon's actions can be called centrifugal, since he became famous for his victories (as well as defeats) that carried the spirit of a new times started by the French Revolution; on the other hand, the main achievement of Emperor Haile Sellassie was the defense of Ethiopia from Italian fascists: that is, his actions were centripetal, directed at the defense of traditional interests and the culture of his country.

It is not surprising that the Crown prince exists on the photograph in his own special space: he is entirely different compared to the common people. He is not just a nobleman; he exists, to some extent, on the level of mysticism and legends since he traces his origin to King Solomon and the Queen of Sheba. It is also extremely important to note that although the photographic space is created by the photographer, it turns out to be captured and appropriated by the photographed. By hanging the backdrop

---

11   Barthes, p.13.

and spreading the carpet on the ground Gumilev separated Tafari from concrete African space, and created for him his own, almost speculative, deliberately flattened space in which the prince reigns, towering in the center like a pyramid. At the same time the photograph is not static. The fold in the backdrop forms a diagonal line that runs from the lower left corner to the upper right corner. The diagonal creates the sense of Tafari's movement forward toward the viewer and of soaring upward (the effect is made even stronger since we do not see the feet of the person photographed because they are hidden by his shama). This movement forward connects our space with the photographic space possessed by the subject, the movement upward maintains the independence of the photographed space from the infringements of the photographer and, through him, from our infringements.

A similar flattened, speculative space, occupied and dominated by the subject, can be found in the remarkable photograph of Abyssinian noblemen with a servant Shankella boy. The entire photographic space is filled by just their faces, but at the same time it represents the structure of the Abyssinian landscape as it is perceived by its inhabitants with unbelievable fullness. The structure is created by three gazes that form the semantic vectors of the photograph's space: the servant boy looks down behind the backs of his masters, the left Abyssinian raises his eyes to the sky, and the one on the right looks straight at the viewer. Once again, we face a special space that possesses almost mystical depth in spite of its flatness, or, perhaps, precisely because of it. The boy's downward look from under his semi-closed eyelids defines the rear and lower plane of the space located behind the backs of his masters, the "Abyssinian knights."[12] This space is concealed from us, the outside viewers. We can say that it is *their* space, in which they exist and which they shield and defend from outside encroachments. The upward gaze of the Abyssinian on the left opens the photographic space up, providing it with an outlet and indicating an aspiration for the sky, for the spiritual world. The gaze of the Abyssinian on the right, directed straight at us, connects us to the photographic space and at the same time warns against merging with it, making it independent from our intrusion. The gun on the boy's shoulder directed upward stresses the same idea of defending this space and, on the

---

12   N. Gumilev, "Afrikanskii dnevnik," in Nikolai Gumilev's *Sobranie sochinenii v trekh tomakh*, v. 3 (Moscow: Xudozh. literatura, 1991), p. 283.

other hand, intensifies the striving upward, repeating the directed gaze of the Abyssinian on the left.

The three faces themselves resemble a landscape with mighty mountains (Abyssinia was called the "roof of the world"), valleys, and precipices. Thus, the photograph becomes a body, a living organism. In the process of our examination, it transforms into the photographed people and places, not a "flat death," as Roland Barthes referred to photography, but what we can call a "flat life."

In his photographs, Gumilev manages to avoid condescension, which was characteristic for common Europeans views of Africa determined by their personal and social specificity (expressed as a rule through a neutral, anonymous third person perspective). Unlike his European contemporaries, Gumilev overcomes to some degree the cultural gap between the European photographer and the inhabitants of Ethiopia whom he photographed (a gap which, no matter how paradoxical it may seem, became even wider after the emergence of post-colonial theory).

We can discern three clearly delineated cultural planes in the discussed photographs, the planes formed between the depicted reality, Nikolai Gumilev, and us: 1) "then-present" plane of the depicted; 2) "then-present" plane of the photographer (that is, N. Gumilev); and 3) "now-present" plane of the researcher that serves as a kind of a substitute for the real experience of a contemporary viewer. Or, perhaps, there are only two planes: the relationship between the photographer and the photographed and the relationship between the photograph and us today, both merging together on the pages of the present paper.

Gumilev's and Sverchkov's photographs suggest a dialogue, an exchange between I/eye (the photographer) and You (people and objects photographed by me/him and also the viewers). The cultural distance between the photographer and the photographed, between the white and the native, narrows. The photographed space becomes the space of the photographer. He seemingly settles in it, achieving in this way that understanding of the photographed landscape which Barthes considered to be its essence: "For me, a landscape photograph (urban or rural) must be inhabitable, and not simply visited. This desire to settle in… is not oneric… and not empirical,… it is phantasmatic, originating on some kind of a second level which, it seems, carried me forward into a utopian time or back to something in myself: the double movement which Baudelaire celebrated in *Invitation au voyage* and *La Vie anterieure*, it is as though I was *sure* in what was that or traveled there".[13]

So, where does Gumilev travel to and where does he dwell when he enters the African landscape of his photographs? Susan Sontag has observed that "Photography is a thin slice of both space and time."[14] Photography theorists point out that photography is inevitably connected to the past. As Laszlo Moholy-Nagy writes, "photography... can help to reconstruct the spatial spirit of the past."[15] In his introduction to "The African Hunt," Gumilev writes:

> A European... may see the Africa of thousands of years ago: nameless rivers with heavy, leaden waves, deserts where it seems only God dares to raise his voice, forests, which are totally rotted through and are ready to fall from a single push, hidden in mountain canyons...[16]

Gumilev indicates that his trip to Africa is a return to the past, to the sources of life, the primeval, primal principle of existence. Gumilev thus perceives the African landscape as a feminine body. In the same introduction to "The African Hunt" he says:

> On ancient vignettes, Africa was often represented as a young woman who was beautiful despite the coarse simplicity of her forms, and she was always, always surrounded by wild beasts. Monkeys swinging over her head, elephants waving their trunks behind her back, a lion licking her feet, a panther luxuriating next to her on a cliff warmed by the sun.[17]

Undoubtedly it is an allegorical image with all conventions of its times. However, coupled with the return to the past and stressing the

---

13 Barthes, p. 38.
14 Sontag, p. 22.
15 László Moholy-Nagy, "Space" in *Poetics of Space. A Critical Photographic Anthology*, ed. by Steve Yates, Albuquerque: University of New Mexico Press, 1994, p. 151.
16 N. Gumilev, "Afrikanskaia okhota," in Nikolai Gumilev's *Sobranie sochinenii v trekh tomakh*, v. 2 (Moscow: Xudozh. literatura, 1991), p. 223.
17 *Ibid.*, p. 221.

"primordiality" of the "woman Africa," we can say that the African landscape is feminine and, as we will see below, emphatically maternal.

I begin the discussion of this theme with the photograph of Dejazmach Tafari's wife, which was taken at the same time as that of her husband.

> Then it was the princess' turn, his wife. She was a sister of the liege Iyasu, the heir to the throne, and consequently, a granddaughter of Menelik. She was twenty-two, three years older than her husband, and the features of her face were very pleasant, in spite of a certain fullness which had already spoiled her figure. However, it seemed that she was expecting. The Dejazmach paid the most touching attention to her. He himself sat her in the requisite pose, straightened her dress, and asked us to take her picture several times in order that they would be sure to turn out... We took the picture of the princess with her two girl servants.[18]

As in the portrait of her husband, the princess is shown as a ruler. She stands, towering in the center of the picture, with her hands on the shoulders of her servants. That was that effect which her husband probably tried to evoke. He was also the creator of her photographic space. However, that space did not submit to either his or the photographer's will. It comes out as a purely feminine space filled with women's bodies and itself becomes such. Moreover, it becomes a maternal space because the servant girls can be perceived as a visual realization of the fetus, concealed in the womb of the princess; that is, the space acquires the meaning that Barthes discusses in reference to Freud: "Now Freud speaks about a maternal body which 'represents the only place of which one can say with complete assurance that you/we have already been there.' Such would be the essence of a landscape (willingly chosen): *heimlich*, awaking Mother in me...."[19]

In this respect, it is interesting to consider the cycle of photographs taken during Gumilev's visit to a town built on the place where the prophet Sheik-Hussein lived. "...then after a heavy sleep we photographed the book and the town,"[20] Gumilev wrote in his diary. Among the photographs, the most important include one of a stone that, according to legend,

---

18   N. Gumilev, "Afrikanskii dnevnik," p. 280
19   Barthes, p. 38.
20   Quoted in V. V. Bronguleev, *Posredine stranstviia zemnogo.*

Sheik-Hussein turned a woman into, as well as the photograph of the entrance to the cave where Sheik-Hussein lived, which represents an entrance to the bosom, the womb of the woman earth. In this context, the photograph of Gumilev himself, standing among the rocks, is read with a new meaning. On the photograph, Gumilev almost merges with the surrounding landscape. He becomes inscribed in it and is not immediately noticeable: his black cape blends with the outline of the rocks, and his helmet looks like a protruding stone. Gumilev also becomes part of his photographs in the literal sense of the word. Some of his photographs bear imprints of fingers of those who developed them. Thus Gumilev's body becomes a physical part of the photographic landscape, which in turn can be seen as a materialized maternal body. In other words, Gumilev returns to the mother's bosom, which, according to Barthes, is located in the center of life's labyrinth.

A special place among the photographs taken at Sheik-Hussein belongs to the photographs of Sheik-Hussein's book that Gumilev holds in his hands, turning its pages. Susan Sontag observes the following on the nature of photography: "Reality itself has started to be understood as a kind of writing, which has to be decoded - even as photographed images were themselves first compared to writing... Fox Talbot called the camera 'the pencil of nature.'"[21] What is this book if not a prophet's words, the words of his prayers and incantations as a result of which the surrounding landscape comes into being: the stone woman, stone fingers, the man-tree, etc. Here the material truthfulness of photography turns into myth. "Perhaps, we possess an insuperable resistance to the belief in the past, in History, except those cases when it appears as myth," Barthes writes. "Photography... ends this resistance: in it the past becomes as definite as the present; what we see on paper is as definite as what we touch."[22] On a photograph we see reality as simultaneously the past and the present.

Roland Barthes indicates the context of the photographic vision of the world: "To see oneself on the scale of History."[23] In this context, a photograph (or more precisely the space represented on that photograph

---

Dokumental'naia povest' o zhizni i tvorchestve Nikolaia Gumileva. Gody 1886-1913 (Moscow: Mysl', 1995), p. 332.
21   Sontag, p. 160
22   Barthes, p. 87.
23   *Ibid.*, p. 12.

and the person inscribed into that space) acquires mythic forms, the "mythological status... as a kind of a materialized memory trace, deeply deposited in the context of personal associations and private 'perspectives.'"[24]

In this context, Barthes calls early photographers mythographers and says that a photographer reminds him of "Orpheus in the sense that he should not turn around to take a look at what he leads, what he gives me,"[25] (that is, the viewer). The Orpheus in Gumilev presents us with a mythologized African landscape that consists of its inhabitants merging with the space inhabited by them and includes the space of the photographer: that is, the Orpheus who despite all the warnings nevertheless turned around to look at it.

– Slava I. Yastremski
Professor of Russian Bucknell University

---

24   *Ibid.*, p. 12.
25   R. Barthes, "The Photographic Message," in *Image/Music/Text*, p.19.

THE PHOTOGRAPHS FROM THE GUMILEV AFRICA EXPEDITIONS

Captions of the following photographs marked with an asterisk are translations from Russian of jottings on prints describing the content of individual prints provided for this volume. Captions without an asterisk are provided to describe the generic contents of pictures.

Southern slopes of the Errer Mountains *

Plowing with bulls in the provinces of Morocco *

Camel crossing on the Kassam River in Abyssinia (Ethiopia) *

Waterfall from the cliffs of the Errer Mountains in Adda *

Portrait of older
bearded man

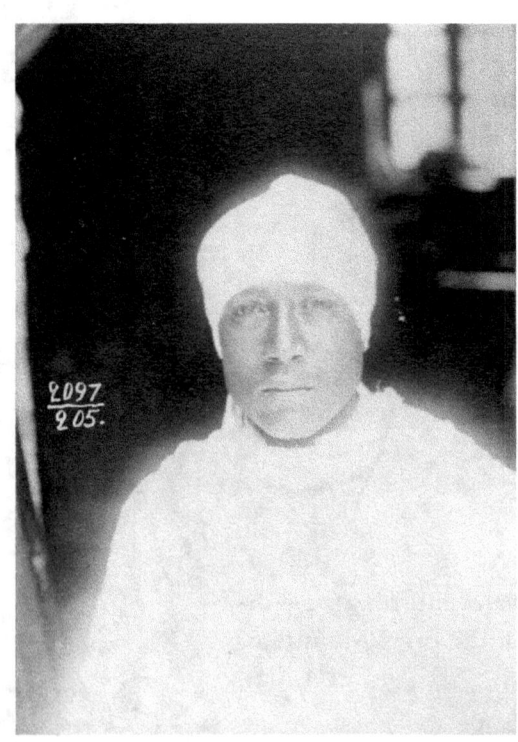

Portrait of noble young
Abyssinian man *

Father and sons

Abyssinian mother
with her child

Russians with local inhabitants

Portrait of man

Market scene

Man smoking a water pipe

Older man sitting

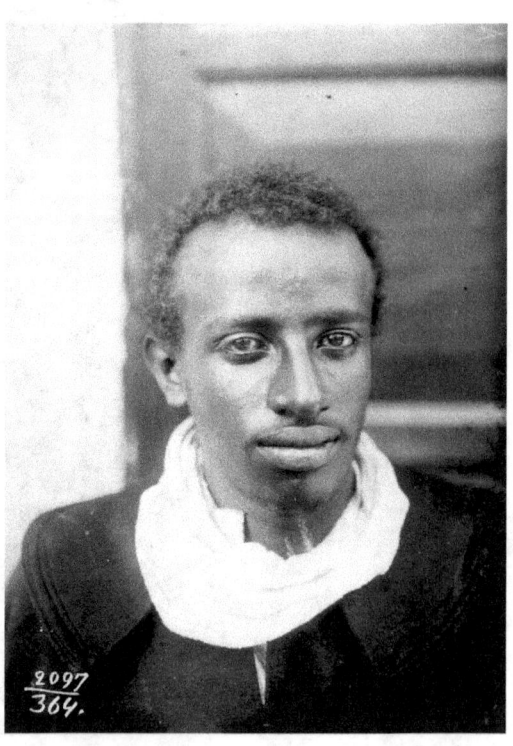

Close-up of man

Winnowing of grain in a Galla village
in the steppe part of the upper Auash *

Man with rifle

Russians posing
beneath a baobab tree

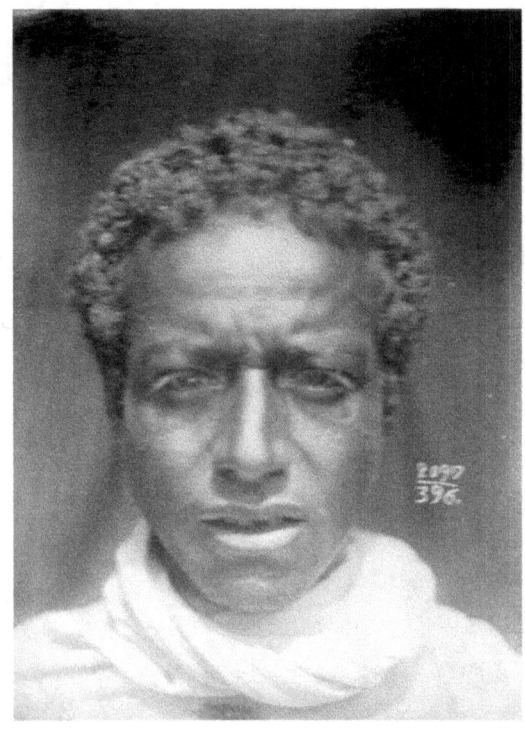

Close-up of a man

Russian men next to bushes

Tree

Ashker - a Galla standing near a tree *

Thatched-roof house

Nikolai Borgarin underneath a cactus in Morocco *

Mountainous landscape *

Man plowing with oxen

Three men standing with spears

Russian medical personnel with local assistants

Men gathered in village for a celebration

Men gathered by stream possibly for a baptism

Men dancing and singing to drumbeat

Orthodox priests

Noble woman seated with daughters and others in retinue

Three young girls

Princess and future Empress Menen Asfaw (wife of Haile Selassie) with retinue

Trees

Men in front of thatched roof building

Men running with rifles

Russian men on horseback in rocky terrain

Village scene

Men gathered in village

Southern slopes of the Errer Mountains *

Woman next to stone wall

Woman in robe near thatched-roof house

Portrait of bearded man standing

Orthodox priest in vestments

Portrait of father and son in front of stone wall

Ashker (servant) with rifle

Men with rifles accompanying Emperor Menelik II

Men gathered with drummers for celebration

Man in white wrap

VIP surrounded by men

Emperor Menelik II posing with Russian military officials

Gallas at a bazaar *

VIP wearing hat on horseback with men armed with rifles

Landscape

Inhabitants of Baroda *

Danakils

Landscape with stream

Landscape

Graveyard

Rock outcropping

The Sacred Book of Sheikh Hussein

Rock formation

Tree near tent

Huts with villagers

Train cars by trees in field

Ravine with rocks

Encampment

Village scene

Man in turban

Gumilev transcribing Abyssinian folk song

Close-up of man by wall

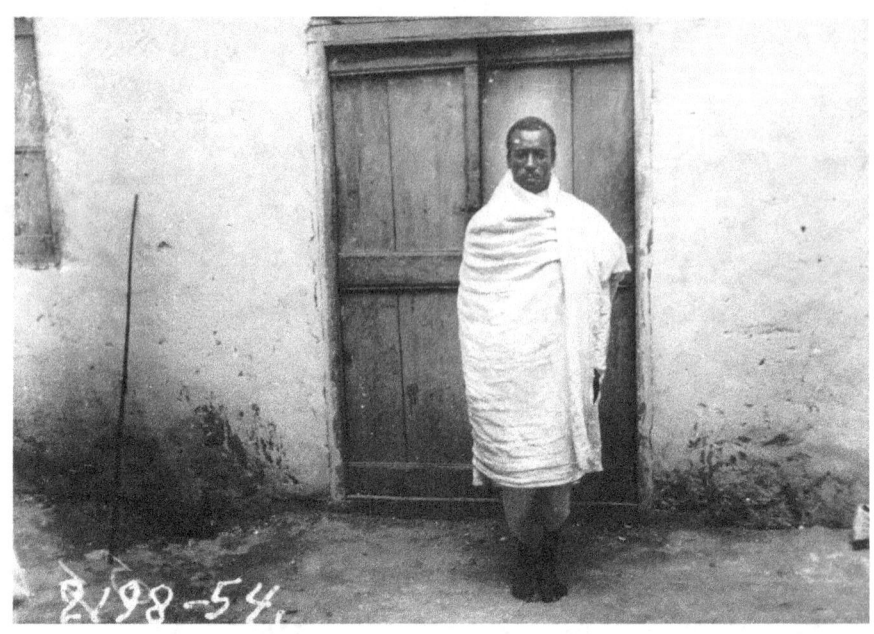

Abyssinian man standing by door

Lone tree landscape

Stone pillar with other rocks

Two Russian men eating from woven basket

Man weaving on loom

Family with children

Nikolai Gumilev near rock outcroppings

Man walking with horse

Road into woods

Clearing with trees

Close-up of man

Close-up of man in profile

Close-up of cliffs

Tafari Makonnen (the future Emperor Haile Selassie) *

Close-up of older Harari woman in profile

Close-up of older Harari woman with flower in her hair

Young woman walking in profile

Three men in a field

Gnarled tree

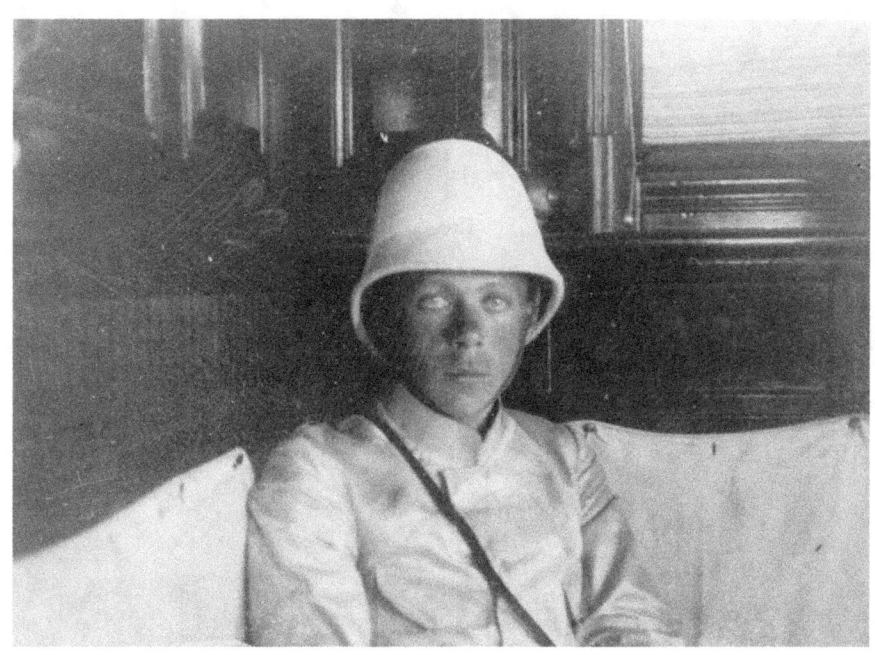

Gumilev's nephew and cameraman Nikolai Sverchkov *

Large stone

Three men near their tent

Men on trail with packhorse

Nikolai Gumilev with man

The sacred book of Sheikh Hussein, a town in southeast Abyssinia/Ethiopia sacred to Muslims and named after the thirteenth-century religious figure Sheikh Hussein, who introduced Islam to the Sidamo people

The sacred book of Sheikh Hussein

Postcard dated August 15, 1913

Милая Оля! Поздравляю тебя съ праздникомъ Рождества Христова, дай Богъ чтобы встрѣтить и провести его въ радости и добромъ здоровьѣ. Полѣзать къ тебѣ хотѣлось бы, да семью неосавишь, а главное дѣтей. Я себя чувствую плохо, первое лѣто отъ растоянiе съ мужемъ большiе мѣста. Много онъ сулѣ ведя своей носъ и много подвезлѣ себя при дѣтяхъ а ту тоже сказываетъ на нихъ, по отношенiю ко мнѣ много стали задерживаютъ, а особенно Нина. Коля и Серенса еще имѣютъ любовь и жалѣютъ меня. Учатся всѣ хорошо, Коля въ эту четверть получилъ три, два тройки, а Серенел игр... неодна похуже другихъ. Им Мама здорова и поздравляетъ скоро напишу ...

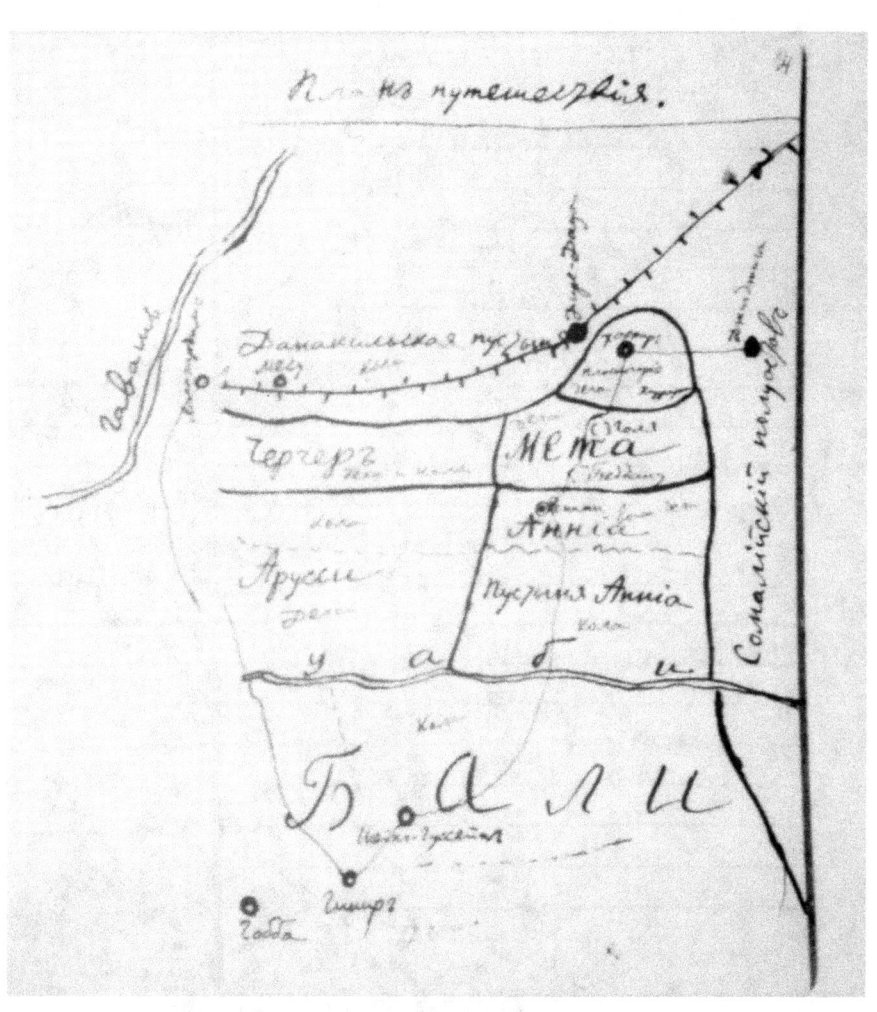

Map in Russian of planned travel route

Emperor Menelik II meets with Russian military delegation

A Brown Man in Russia - Perambulations Through A Siberian Winter
by Vijay Menon

A Brown Man in Russia describes the fantastical travels of a young, colored American traveler as he backpacks across Russia in the middle of winter via the Trans-Siberian. The book is a hybrid between the curmudgeonly travelogues of Paul Theroux and the philosophical works of Robert Pirsig. Styled in the vein of Hofstadter, the author lays out a series of absurd, but true stories followed by a deeper rumination on what they mean and why they matter. Each chapter presents a vivid anecdote from the perspective of the fumbling traveler and concludes with a deeper lesson to be gleaned. For those who recognize the discordant nature of our world in a time ripe for demagoguery and for those who want to make it better, the book is an all too welcome antidote. It explores the current global climate of despair over differences and outputs a very different message – one of hope and shared understanding. At times surreal, at times inappropriate, at times hilarious, and at times deeply human, A Brown Man in Russia is a reminder to those who feel marginalized, hopeless, or endlessly divided that harmony is achievable even in the most unlikely of places.

Buy it > www.glagoslav.com

The Flying Dutchman
by Anatoly Kudryavitsky

Some time in the 1970s, Konstantin Alpheyev, a well-known Russian musicologist, finds himself in trouble with the KGB, the Russian secret police, after the death of his girlfriend, for which one of their officers may have been responsible. He has to flee from the city and to go into hiding. He rents an old house located on the bank of a big Russian river, and lives there like a recluse observing nature and working on his new book about Wagner. The house, a part of an old barge, undergoes strange metamorphoses rebuilding itself as a medieval schooner, and Alpheyev begins to identify himself with the Flying Dutchman. Meanwhile, the police locate his new whereabouts and put him under surveillance. A chain of strange events in the nearby village makes the police officer contact the KGB, and the latter figure out who the new tenant of the old house actually is.

Buy it > www.glagoslav.com

Leo Tolstoy – Flight from Paradise
by Pavel Basinsky

Over a hundred years ago, something truly outrageous occurred at Yasnaya Polyana. Count Leo Tolstoy, a famous author aged eighty-two at the time, took off, destination unknown. Since then, the circumstances surrounding the writer's whereabouts during his final days and his eventual death have given rise to many myths and legends. In this book, popular Russian writer and reporter Pavel Basinsky delves into the archives and presents his interpretation of the situation prior to Leo Tolstoy's mysterious disappearance. Basinsky follows Leo Tolstoy throughout his life, right up to his final moments. Reconstructing the story from historical documents, he creates a visionary account of the events that led to the Tolstoys' family drama.

Flight from Paradise will be of particular interest to international researchers studying Leo Tolstoy's life and works, and is highly recommended to a broader audience worldwide.

Buy it > www.glagoslav.com

Dear Reader,

Thank you for purchasing this book.

We at Glagoslav Publications are glad to welcome you, and hope that you find our books to be a source of knowledge and inspiration.

We want to show the beauty and depth of the Slavic region to everyone looking to expand their horizon and learn something new about different cultures, different people, and we believe that with this book we have managed to do just that.

Now that you've got to know us, we want to get to know you. We value communication with our readers and want to hear from you! We offer several options:

– Join our Book Club on Goodreads, Library Thing and Shelfari, and receive special offers and information about our giveaways;

– Share your opinion about our books on Amazon, Barnes & Noble, Waterstones and other bookstores;

– Join us on Facebook and Twitter for updates on our publications and news about our authors;

– Visit our site www.glagoslav.com to check out our Catalogue and subscribe to our Newsletter.

Glagoslav Publications is getting ready to release a new collection and planning some interesting surprises — stay with us to find out!

Glagoslav Publications
Email: contact@glagoslav.com

Glagoslav Publications Catalogue

- *The Time of Women* by Elena Chizhova
- *Andrei Tarkovsky: The Collector of Dreams* by Layla Alexander-Garrett
- *Andrei Tarkovsky - A Life on the Cross* by Lyudmila Boyadzhieva
- *Sin* by Zakhar Prilepin
- *Hardly Ever Otherwise* by Maria Matios
- *Khatyn* by Ales Adamovich
- *The Lost Button* by Irene Rozdobudko
- *Christened with Crosses* by Eduard Kochergin
- *The Vital Needs of the Dead* by Igor Sakhnovsky
- *The Sarabande of Sara's Band* by Larysa Denysenko
- *A Poet and Bin Laden* by Hamid Ismailov
- *Watching The Russians (Dutch Edition)* by Maria Konyukova
- *Kobzar* by Taras Shevchenko
- *The Stone Bridge* by Alexander Terekhov
- *Moryak* by Lee Mandel
- *King Stakh's Wild Hunt* by Uladzimir Karatkevich
- *The Hawks of Peace* by Dmitry Rogozin
- *Harlequin's Costume* by Leonid Yuzefovich
- *Depeche Mode* by Serhii Zhadan
- *The Grand Slam and other stories (Dutch Edition)* by Leonid Andreev
- *METRO 2033 (Dutch Edition)* by Dmitry Glukhovsky
- *METRO 2034 (Dutch Edition)* by Dmitry Glukhovsky
- *A Russian Story* by Eugenia Kononenko
- *Herstories, An Anthology of New Ukrainian Women Prose Writers*
- *The Battle of the Sexes Russian Style* by Nadezhda Ptushkina
- *A Book Without Photographs* by Sergey Shargunov
- *Down Among The Fishes* by Natalka Babina
- *disUNITY* by Anatoly Kudryavitsky
- *Sankya* by Zakhar Prilepin
- *Wolf Messing* by Tatiana Lungin
- *Good Stalin* by Victor Erofeyev

- *Solar Plexus* by Rustam Ibragimbekov
- *Don't Call me a Victim!* by Dina Yafasova
- *Poetin (Dutch Edition)* by Chris Hutchins and Alexander Korobko
- *A History of Belarus* by Lubov Bazan
- *Children's Fashion of the Russian Empire* by Alexander Vasiliev
- *Empire of Corruption - The Russian National Pastime* by Vladimir Soloviev
- *Heroes of the 90s - People and Money. The Modern History of Russian Capitalism*
- *Fifty Highlights from the Russian Literature (Dutch Edition)* by Maarten Tengbergen
- *Bajesvolk (Dutch Edition)* by Mikhail Khodorkovsky
- *Tsarina Alexandra's Diary (Dutch Edition)*
- *Myths about Russia* by Vladimir Medinskiy
- *Boris Yeltsin - The Decade that Shook the World* by Boris Minaev
- *A Man Of Change - A study of the political life of Boris Yeltsin*
- *Sberbank - The Rebirth of Russia's Financial Giant* by Evgeny Karasyuk
- *To Get Ukraine* by Oleksandr Shyshko
- *Asystole* by Oleg Pavlov
- *Gnedich* by Maria Rybakova
- *Marina Tsvetaeva - The Essential Poetry*
- *Multiple Personalities* by Tatyana Shcherbina
- *The Investigator* by Margarita Khemlin
- *The Exile* by Zinaida Tulub
- *Leo Tolstoy – Flight from paradise* by Pavel Basinsky
- *Moscow in the 1930* by Natalia Gromova
- *Laurus (Dutch edition)* by Evgenij Vodolazkin
- *Prisoner* by Anna Nemzer
- *The Crime of Chernobyl - The Nuclear Goulag* by Wladimir Tchertkoff
- *Alpine Ballad* by Vasil Bykau
- *The Complete Correspondence of Hryhory Skovoroda*

- *The Tale of Aypi* by Ak Welsapar
- *Selected Poems* by Lydia Grigorieva
- *The Fantastic Worlds of Yuri Vynnychuk*
- *The Garden of Divine Songs and Collected Poetry of Hryhory Skovoroda*
- *Adventures in the Slavic Kitchen: A Book of Essays with Recipes*
- *Seven Signs of the Lion* by Michael M. Naydan
- *Forefathers' Eve* by Adam Mickiewicz
- *One-Two* by Igor Eliseev
- *Girls, be Good* by Bojan Babić
- *Time of the Octopus* by Anatoly Kucherena
- *The Grand Harmony* by Bohdan Ihor Antonych
- *The Selected Lyric Poetry Of Maksym Rylsky*
- *The Shining Light* by Galymkair Mutanov
- *The Frontier: 28 Contemporary Ukrainian Poets - An Anthology*
- *Acropolis - The Wawel Plays* by Stanisław Wyspiański
- *Contours of the City* by Attyla Mohylny
- *Conversations Before Silence: The Selected Poetry of Oles Ilchenko*
- *The Secret History of my Sojourn in Russia* by Jaroslav Hašek
- *Mirror Sand - An Anthology of Russian Short Poems in English Translation* (A Bilingual Edition)
- *Maybe We're Leaving* by Jan Balaban
- *A Brown Man in Russia - Perambulations Through A Siberian Winter* by Vijay Menon
- *Death of the Snake Catcher* by Ak Welsapar
- *Hard Times* by Ostap Vyshnia
- *Vladimir Lenin - How to Become a Leader* by Vladlen Loginov
- *Soghomon Tehlirian Memories - The Assassination of Talaat*
- *Duel* by Borys Antonenko-Davydovych
- *Zinnober's Poppets* by Elena Chizhova
- *The Hemingway Game* by Evgeni Grishkovets
- *The Nuremberg Trials* by Alexander Zvyagintsev
- *Mikhail Bulgakov - The Life and Times* by Marietta Chudakova

More coming soon...

www.ingramcontent.com/pod-product-compliance
Lightning Source LLC
Chambersburg PA
CBHW071340080526
44587CB00017B/2907